ABOUT THE AUTHOR

Ben Renshaw is an inspirational speaker, seminar leader, success coach and broadcaster. He is co-director of The Happiness Project, working with leaders in business, health and education. A former classical violinist, his role today is in helping people fulfil their potential. He lives in London with his wife Veronica.

Also by Ben Renshaw

Successful But Something Missing

TOGETHER
BUT
SOMETHING
MISSING

How to create and sustain
successful relationships

Ben Renshaw

LONDON • SYDNEY • AUCKLAND • JOHANNESBURG

1 3 5 7 9 10 8 6 4 2

First published in 2001 by Vermilion,
an imprint of Ebury Press, Random House, 20 Vauxhall Bridge Road, London
SW1V 2SA

Random House Australia (Pty) Limited
20 Alfred Street, Milsons Point, Sydney,
New South Wales 2061, Australia

Random House New Zealand Limited
18 Poland Road, Glenfield,
Auckland 10, New Zealand

Random House South Africa (Pty) Limited
Endulini, 5A Jubilee Road,
Parktown 2193, South Africa

The Random House Group Limited Reg. No. 954009

Printed and bound by Mackays of Chatham plc, Kent

A CIP catalogue record for this book is available from the British Library

ISBN 0-0918-5593-4

Dedicated to Veronica
Thank you for sharing the journey.

Contents

Acknowledgements

This book is made possible by the amazing support I received. Thank you to my mother, Virginia, for your insight, dedication and love. Thank you to my father, Peter, for believing in me. Thank you to my sister, Sophie, for being there. Thank you to Robert Holden, your wisdom and friendship is an inspiration. Thank you to Candy Constable for your staying power. Thank you to all the helpers and participants at The Happiness Project. Thank you to Nick Williams, your friendship is invaluable. Thank you to the team at myhotel, what a great place for relationships. Thank you to my editor Judith Kendra, your expertise is greatly appreciated.

Note: Every case history in this book is included with the consent of those involved. Names have been altered where requested.

ACKNOWLEDGEMENTS

Introduction

Have you longed to know how to navigate a relationship successfully? As I set out to find the path, I discovered that the essential ingredient is the understanding that a relationship is a journey and not a destination. By putting in the right kind of work, you determine how you travel along the way. To see a relationship as a river and to be prepared to go with the current, flowing over boulders and stones, means that you stop struggling upstream. A relationship is a constant source of adventure, opportunity, excitement and growth, which makes life deeply rewarding.

We all have relationship problems, although I'm sure that we do not consciously set out to have hard times. Problems arise because that is in the nature of a relationship, but whilst you cannot eliminate problems, you can relate to them in a different way. The sooner you give up the illusion that you will never have another relationship problem, the sooner your relationship will be a success. The key is to get excited about the problems that you face, to accept them wholeheartedly as part of the human experience, and to welcome the learning that they bring.

If you are not sufficiently challenged in a relationship you lose interest; equally if it becomes too challenging you look for an exit route. To get the balance right requires you to find a middle path. *Together But Something Missing* acts as a compass pointing you in the right direction and guiding you when you get off track.

The book derives from my background in psychology, my work with clients, and most importantly my compassion. I have always been a people person and that passion drives me today to have faith in relationships. With the breakdown of the nuclear family, new social trends are emerging. The form may be different, however the intrinsic desire to enjoy an intimate, loving relationship is as strong as ever.

Despite all our advances in technology and information,

nothing can replace the significance of a relationship. No matter how sophisticated your computer, how full your bank account, how many air miles you have clocked up, or how successful your business; the need for unconditional love, deep companionship, sexual intimacy and to be understood is as timeless as the rising and setting of the sun.

It is essential that you make your relationship a priority. In this age of 'busyness' and 'hurry sickness' it's easy to take it for granted, neglecting the very thing that can give life so much meaning and joy. Reading this book is a reflection of your commitment to rectify this balance. It celebrates your ability to create love and understanding, and to put an end to the feeling that something is missing. Let it inspire you to renew your trust, to start afresh and to create an extraordinary relationship which will fulfil you on a soul level.

1

The Past is Past

I awoke early one morning with a mixture of nerves and excitement – it was my wedding day. Three weeks earlier I had returned from New Zealand, the home of Veronica, my fiancée, where we had celebrated our engagement with her family and friends. We'd originally planned that our wedding would take place in about two years with both our families present, but after this trip we decided not to wait. I called up our local Register Office in Chelsea and made the booking. It would mean that Veronica's family was unable to be present, but we had their blessing and all was well.

As I put on my wedding suit I laughed to myself. I couldn't quite believe it. The doubts that I had about marriage, my vows that I wouldn't get married for at least another ten years, the impossibility that I would meet someone to share my life with had all gone out the window. My past relationship experience did not lend itself to marriage. I had suffered the pain of rejection, heartbreaks and losses. I had enjoyed my bachelor status, finding it secure and hassle-free. I had watched my own parents' marriage end and witnessed countless relationship breakdowns at great cost to all involved. I realised that if I let my relationship history repeat itself it would be a disaster.

I had my oldest friend Doug navigate the London traffic to arrive at the Register Office on time. He was a good person to have at my side; already married and divorced, he was familiar with the procedure. Seeing the faces of family and friends was a reassuring feeling. We completed the last-minute procedures and took our place in front of the Registrar. He had a good sense of humour and joked that this was just another day at the office. Not in my world! I will never forget the moment when he turned to me and asked if I would take Veronica Therese Annan to be my lawfully wedded wife. The time had arrived. I was struck with emotion. A mixture of tears and laughter welled up inside me. I couldn't catch my breath. I was handed a box of Kleenex and told to breathe deeply. Finding my voice I said the ancient words, 'Yes, I do'. In that moment I felt myself letting go of past fears and doubts as I experienced an overwhelming sense of peace and strength. This was it. A new chapter of my life that I never thought would be possible had begun.

We have all had powerful experiences in relationships, which have accelerated the letting go of the past; in particular, the disappointments, grievances and wounds, which limit our relationships today. Learning to put the past in the past on a daily basis allows us to fulfil our relationship potential now. Within each of us exists an inner torch for love, intimacy and joy; but its flame dims when the past dominates our present. This chapter shows you how to let go of the past so that it no longer influences your relationships in unhelpful ways, whilst giving you insights that place you firmly on the path to creating relationship intelligence.

Letting your past be history

See if the following scenarios are familiar to you:

- Relationships are difficult. They never work out. Men won't commit. Women are too needy. It's just too complicated.
- I'm trying to balance my working life with a relationship, and it's proving a struggle. There just don't seem to be enough hours in a day and both suffer as a consequence.
- We were constantly irritating each other, arguing over right/wrong issues, trying to dominate the relationship. I left to begin a new one. Several months later I was back to where I started – same problems, different person.
- All women want to do is shop. Their appetite is insatiable.

However much money I save she eventually spends it.
◈ A man's life is sport. They are either watching it or playing it. Where do I fit in?

These are some of the most common relationship dilemmas that I encounter in my work. I believe that you could go up to anyone, anywhere in the world and say, 'I'm sorry to hear about your relationship problems', and they would exclaim, 'how did you know!'

The source of relationship difficulties is rooted in the past. *Anything unresolved from past relationships influences present ones.* However, your relationship history does not have to be your relationship destiny. By recognising past unhelpful habits you immediately create an opening for new possibilities, and by making the decision to let your past be history you enable yourself to take a major step away from it.

In the journey of resolving the past do not be surprised if you experience an initial resistance to letting it go. We are creatures of habit and move towards what is familiar. This explains why we tend to recreate the same relationship scenarios, even if they don't support us. We also associate letting go with a sense of loss, which makes us reluctant to move on. However, we cannot lose anything of real value to us and unhelpful habits have no value.

I once worked with a client called Sue who is an example of how the past can dominate current relationships. She claimed that she always seemed to attract the same type of men. She said that the first six months were great, but as soon as they became more intimate, the men backed off. I asked about her family history. She disclosed that her father had left her mother when she was six months old. As a result her mother used to tell her that men couldn't be trusted and that they were afraid of commitment. Sue had been influenced by this message and formed an unconscious blueprint that the men she loved would leave her. This became a self-fulfilling prophecy and each rejection she experienced confirmed her belief even more.

Another example is the case of Amanda, who felt that she made the wrong choices in her relationships. She found it impossible to commit due to the constant questioning in her mind. When we explored the issue she realised that she felt wrong as a woman and projected that perception on to her relationships. Amanda wanted to get to the bottom of it and was prepared to ask her parents if anything had occurred that might have created this dynamic. As she was the third child with two elder sisters I suggested that maybe they had wanted a boy at her birth. Upon asking them if this was the case, they reassured her that their major concern had been that she was healthy. At a later date Amanda found some old christening letters sent to her mother, which stated, 'better luck next time'. Clearly, they had wanted a boy after all.

How do you know if your past is dominating your current relationships? A good indication is if you continue to have the same recurring problems. When you are having a difficult time, ask yourself: *'What am I holding on to from the past?' 'What are the major messages I received that influence my relationships in unhelpful ways today?'* Whether they are connected with family issues or previous relationships, becoming aware of these factors allows you to let your past be history.

We all have a story that governs our relationships. For some it's a story of pain and rejection. For others it's a story of dissatisfaction and a lack of fulfilment. Whatever your story, it is up to you how much you choose to identify with it. In truth it is simply a story that you have authored, which you now have the opportunity to rewrite. In doing so you create a new relationship future.

One definition of madness is *'doing the same thing whilst expecting a different result!'* You will continue to do the same thing in your relationships, communicate in the same way and have the same perceptions and expectations until you are willing to let go of your past. When I first entered the world of psychology and personal development my goal was to eliminate my past and to get rid of the excess baggage that I carried. After those initial few years in which I tried to achieve that aim, I changed my focus from 'trying to get rid of my past' to 'accepting it and letting it go'. Your past is not good or bad, right or wrong.

Bringing this understanding and acceptance to it frees you to create a new relationship future.

Resolving the past with your parents

In my workshops I ask participants: *'How many of you would like your relationships to be similar to your parents' relationship?'* The majority answer with a resounding 'No!' The idea of copying our parents' relationship seems a highly unattractive one. Yet, until we become aware of the influence of our parents on our own relationships, we tend to either recreate habits similar to theirs, or rebel and try and do the opposite. Unfortunately neither of these options supports a healthy and loving relationship of our own.

It has become something of a joke that there is no such thing as a functional family. We have all experienced varying degrees of dysfunctional behaviour exhibited by our parents and extended families. (This was highlighted by the popularity of the movie *American Beauty.*) Accepting this fact makes it easier to move away from our past. Instead of trying to change it, we understand that the level of dysfunction was simply a case of people doing their best with the limited resources, psychologically, emotionally and spiritually, that they had at the time. It's extremely rare that a parent consciously sets out to damage a child, but their own unresolved past often becomes transferred on to their offspring.

I observed this when working with Trisha who came to see me having experienced many years of abuse from her father. As a child she was subjected to physical and emotional torment, which left her with deep wounds. As she grew up she played the role of peacemaker in her family by trying to heal the family rifts and getting her father to mend his ways. She never witnessed the changes that she would have liked to see and continued to feel hurt, angry and betrayed. This affected all areas of her life, particularly her own relationships, as she felt unable to trust men or to let them into her life with any degree of intimacy.

When she first disclosed her feelings and experiences from the past I made no comment and contained a space in which she could air her grievances. Since she had invested so much time and energy to no avail in trying to change her father, I knew the importance of listening with empathy before initiating a different point of view. When I began to feel that she had felt truly heard and accepted I encouraged Trisha to reflect on the consequences of her efforts. With difficulty she admitted that nothing had really changed for the better and that she was willing to embrace another perspective. I suggested that she choose to see her father in a different light and that as long as she continued to perceive him as a 'bad, cruel and manipulative man', she would never experience a different outcome in the relationship.

I asked Trisha how she would like to see her father. She said that to view him as a 'kind, whole-hearted, thoughtful and reflective man' was a great challenge for her, but one that she was willing to make. We discussed the role that forgiveness could play, the commitment to letting go of old pain, grievances and revenge and opening the door to empathy, compassion and understanding.

Trisha's willingness to see her father differently, coupled with forgiveness meant that she began to behave differently. She stopped playing the role of peacemaker and learnt to see things from his point of view. She began to understand the pain that he carried from his past. He had also suffered heavy-handed tactics from his father, which had left him scarred. As she continued to approach the relationship in this manner she noticed that his behaviour began to soften and greater opportunity emerged for moments of harmony. Resolving her relationship with her father was a weight lifted off Trisha's shoulders. She felt that she could get on with her own life and develop intimate relationships with men.

It requires courage and support to take the steps that Trisha did, but the cost of holding on to past grievances prevents you from having fully functional relationships now. To recognise that within every upset is a set-up for greater truth, healing and happiness, allows you to set out on the journey of transforming your relationship with your parents.

Paul was another powerful example of someone resolving a parental relationship. In his fifties, he had never met his father who had been an American soldier posted in England during the war. Paul's mother had got pregnant, his father was re-posted and her family refused to allow further contact to be made. His mother went on to marry but Paul never got on with his stepfather. From the age of eighteen, he tried unsuccessfully to trace his father. Many years later he discovered that his mother's family had intercepted all correspondence from his blood father, making it impossible for Paul to locate him. He proceeded to recreate many of the same patterns in his own life, including having no contact with his son from his first marriage following divorce.

In our work together we used a tool known as *completion letters* to resolve his past issues. Completion means to make whole. Writing these letters enables you to heal the fragments and rifts that have occurred between you and your parents. Paul wrote a completion letter to his blood father in which he began to express what he wanted to communicate from his past. The following is what he wrote:

Dear Dad,

It seems strange to write to someone I have never actually met, but I need to communicate my feelings about our relationship. It often feels that you are the part of me that remains shrouded in the mists of time. An aspect of myself that rarely sees the sunshine as it is too scary to bring it forward.

From my understanding of what happened I believe that you did not know of my existence. You brought love and joy to my Mum when she needed it and I was the product of that happy time. It seems that due to my grandmother's fear that Mum may have gone to America with you she intercepted your letters and therefore contact was lost. I am pleased that you were able to share some good times with Mum. No doubt you felt lost and lonely and you must have treasured the time that you shared.

As for myself I have spent time searching for you so that I could discover the part of me that has been a secret. I like to think of you as the child within myself who has forgotten how to play. You are the part of me that has remained constantly innocent throughout my adult life. However, I have carried a lot of anger and pain that has been expressed in many ways, unfortunately not very constructively creating pain and anguish within my family.

It has also been a fairly lonely life as I have found it extremely difficult to allow people to get to know me. I have also found it extremely difficult to trust people. From this position I have alienated myself from my children, in particular my son, who has not spoken to me since he was thirteen.

What I am trying to do now is to break this family cycle to bring back the peace that comes from being able to know that everything is acceptable. I sometimes try to imagine how different things would have been if you had had the opportunity to know me. However, these thoughts of the past only serve to keep me in a time frame that does not support me. Therefore I am attempting to say goodbye to yesterday and hello to the here and now. The past few years have seen me working on myself in an attempt to get to know myself fully. It has been and at times still is, a painful journey of discovery. However, the changes that I have made enable me to share honesty and love in my relationships.

Thank you for listening and who knows I may write again in the future.

I invited him to read the letter aloud to me for the purpose of letting go of the feelings that he still carried. He shed many tears that day as he shared his sense of grief, loss and regret. We then burnt the letter as a symbol of resolution and moving forward. Following this experience Paul began to discover a new level of peace and harmony within himself and his relationships that he claimed was a direct result of his actions.

There is value to be gained in working with completion letters whatever the condition of your relationships. Maybe what you need to express is your love and appreciation or maybe there are unresolved issues from the past, which you can now release. It is important to be patient and compassionate with yourself as you work on the letters.

There are three types of letters to work with. The first version is an angry, blaming letter written solely for your personal healing. Guidelines for writing this letter include the following:

> Dear Mum/Dad,
> What I want to communicate to you is . . .
> What I felt angry about is . . .
> What I felt betrayed about is . . .
> What I felt hurt about is . . .

Read this version to a coach, supportive friend or partner. Burn it or throw it away.

The second version is a forgiveness letter extending compassion and understanding. Prompts include:

> What I am willing to forgive you for is . . .
> What I am willing to see differently is . . .
> What I am willing to understand is . . .
> What I am willing to let go of is . . .

Again, read this to a coach, supportive friend or partner. Burn it or throw it away.

The third and final version is an honest expression of your feelings, in which you communicate with love and understanding the position from the past for the purpose of resolving the relationship. Prompts include:

What I understand is . . .
What I forgive is . . .
What I'm committed to is . . .
What's important is . . .
What I appreciate is . . .
What I love about you is . . .

Check to see if you would feel good about receiving it and read it to a coach, supportive friend or partner for feedback. Send it when you are ready. As we saw in the example with Paul, even if you did not know your blood parent/s, or they are no longer alive, there is great value to be gained from communicating in this manner. When you resolve something for yourself everyone benefits.

Accepting the fact that your parents did the very best job they could with their understanding of parenting is a generous and loving act. It helps to remember that they were the product of their own parenting, which was probably more dysfunctional than yours! They didn't have books to read, therapists to visit and seminars to attend. They were probably too busy trying to survive to be able to have the luxury of reflecting on their own behaviour. Letting your parents off the hook liberates you. It means that you no longer have to change them or change yourself in relation to them. This becomes a new platform for your own relationships, enabling you to enjoy greater love and intimacy.

Letting go of past beliefs

Probably the greatest breakthrough in psychology during the last century was the understanding that whatever our genetic inheritance, we can influence our lives by the choices we make; in particular the beliefs that we choose to hold. Being aware of the past beliefs that you have held about relationships and making new choices today is one of the most powerful methods of transforming your experience of them.

My first major live-in relationship was a struggle. It was hard work. We were stuck in a routine of working hard to survive financially, working hard to keep the relationship afloat, working hard to bridge the gaps in our own families and working hard to have moments of fun. I believed that this was the 'reality' of a relationship. I failed to question the health of it; blindly pressing on, believing that feelings of resentment, unhappiness, sacrifice and suffering were quite natural. On reflection I realise that I expected a relationship to be filled with angst and compromise because that fitted my beliefs at the time. Thankfully, my partner had the wisdom to call it a day. I was devastated at the time because I had taken it for granted that we would be together forever and would struggle together forever. Forever doomed – and I was prepared! Upon reflection, that separation was one of the best things that ever happened to me, because it awoke in me the possibility that there was another path to follow in relationships.

If you have ever experienced continuing sagas of conflict, struggle, win/lose scenarios or any other unhelpful habits in relationships, one of the key points in resolving these issues is to re-evaluate the beliefs that you are choosing to hold about them. You do not have to wait to make new choices. You do not have to wait until you reach the end of this book to make new choices. You do not have to begin a relationship or end one to make new choices. The time to spring clean your beliefs is NOW! The time to make new choices is NOW!

A useful exercise to help you is to write: *my beliefs about relationships are* . . . and to brainstorm what you currently believe to be true. As the principle of beliefs is: *what you believe will be how you live*, the sooner you identify the unhelpful beliefs that you are holding on to, the sooner you can choose new ones that nourish and sustain your relationships.

In my workshops some of the most common unhelpful beliefs revealed by participants include:

◆ Relationships never work out.
◆ You can't trust men – they're all two faced, saying one thing, meaning another.

- The pain of rejection is just too great.
- The fear of intimacy is just too great!
- I feel entrapped.
- I can't be myself in a relationship.
- They're too expensive!
- Sexual attraction gets in the way of true friendship.
- When I'm in love I don't want to work.
- I lose myself in a relationship. I become a 'yes' person when often it goes against my will.
- There could always be someone better around the corner.
- How do I know whether this is the 'right' person?
- They're just too complicated.
- It's easier not to have relationships.
- I get more done when I'm on my own.
- When I'm single I don't have to worry about anyone else.
- I like my independence.
- A relationship cramps my style.
- A relationship is a burden.
- There are too many power games played.

As you can imagine, having a relationship governed by these beliefs would not be much fun. Thankfully, the act of choosing to change a belief does not mean that you have to analyse where it came from, why you have been thinking it and what all its ramifications have been.

The next step is to create a list of beliefs that would nourish and sustain your relationships. Allow these thoughts to uplift and inspire you and move you towards your heart's ideal. Using your creative imagination, write down a list of beliefs to focus on.

These could include:

- My relationships work out for the best for all concerned.
- By trusting myself I can trust others.
- Rejection is nature's way of saying there's a more loving and supportive relationship around the corner.
- Being intimate is a gift to be treasured.

- Freedom is a state of mind that I can carry within a relationship.
- Relationships support me in being true to myself. They enhance my sense of self-worth.
- Sexual attraction adds to real friendship.
- Being in love contributes to my creativity and enjoyment of work.
- Relationships enhance the quality of my life.
- True partnership is a wonderful gift.

It is only natural that when you start to choose new thoughts you are not necessarily going to believe them. This does not mean that they are false; simply that your past belief system is being challenged. You have to allow for a time lag between choosing a new belief and it being 'true' for you.

Watch out for the conversation in your mind that would rather be 'right' about old beliefs than to make new choices. This cynical voice which cries out, 'show me the evidence and then I'll believe it', exhibits backward thinking. It's important to stay flexible in re-evaluating your belief systems. Do not let cynicism stop you from blazing your own trail. You will see the evidence of your new thinking in your relationships because they are an effect of your thoughts.

To ego or not to ego – that is the question!

There is one belief that probably causes more conflict than any other in your relationships – the ego. The ego is no more than an idea that there is something missing. When you project this on to a relationship, you believe that there is something missing within it. This causes you to start looking outside of it for happiness and love. Therefore the ego acts to delay getting what you truly want. It prevents intimacy, inhibits communication, creates fantasy, fuels power struggles, thinks win/lose and celebrates separation.

This dilemma gives rise to one of the greatest challenges in a relationship – the acceptance that it is whole and complete as it is, that there is nothing missing. The motto of the ego is *seek but do not find*. It drives you to keep looking for an ultimate love, an ultimate attraction and an ultimate partner, even when you already might be with that person. It causes you to question, to doubt and to worry when there is nothing to fear. Ask yourself: *how much fear does it take to solve a relationship problem?* No amount of fear will bring you the clarity and peace of mind that you are looking for as long as you are stuck in the ego.

The ego is made of fear and sees itself in everything. According to the ego a relationship is doomed, love is a mistake, intimacy is a life sentence, sex is a performance and honesty is a symptom of insanity! Thankfully, due to our freedom to make choices, we do not have to follow it. Recognising when you are caught in your ego is the first step to undoing it. Perceiving it as just an idea that was formed in nothingness allows it to return to nothingness. Learning to smile at it is another useful strategy (not taking it so seriously), and helps to disarm it.

I watched the ego in action when Ian and Caroline came to see me. They were a well-matched couple who shared similar interests and aims in life. They had a love of the outdoors, enjoyed their respective careers and were looking forward to sharing a life together. They called me after having a series of painful rows. Ian complained that Caroline was criticising his every move, suggesting that he wasn't being loving enough, considerate enough or generous enough. Caroline said that she was feeling rejected. Although Ian said that he loved her and wanted to be with her, his actions appeared to indicate otherwise. Long hours at work and extended sport-watching on television meant that she felt squeezed out.

When we reflected on the situation I asked them to disclose their current fears. Ian admitted that his included loss of identity and independence, having to give up close friendships and not being able to follow his career path. Caroline said that she was afraid of getting hurt, compromising her needs and wants, and being controlled.

I soon realised that taking a logical viewpoint was not going to work. Each time we attempted to analyse the dynamics it ended in another argument. I then explained the role of the ego, trying to undermine the relationship by deflecting the love and empathy. By realising that they had been stuck in an extended attack of the ego they were able to see their situation differently. They strengthened their commitment to transcending it and making new choices each time they were seduced into believing that the fear was real.

Where does the ego dominate in your relationships? Your willingness to admit to its influence catches it off guard. The process of releasing the ego's grip is one of detoxification. It is literally a case of going 'cold turkey' as you cleanse yourself from its hold. Entertain the idea that a happy and peaceful relationship is okay. Since the ego is the great faultfinder, it will look for evidence to show that there is something wrong with your relationship. Take a moment now to remind yourself: there is nothing missing; there is nothing to fear. Saying 'no' to the ego is saying 'yes' to love.

Saying goodbye to past lovers

How often do you catch yourself thinking about old lovers? Do you enjoy the nostalgia that it creates? It is amazing how we perform selective remembering when it comes to past relationships. We tend to focus on the good times and forget why we are no longer with that person. The trouble with staying in the past is that it keeps you out of present time and prevents you from fulfilling your relationship potential now.

Michael and Dawn had been married for ten years by the time they came to see me. They said that passion and intimacy had disappeared. They were constantly arguing over the smallest of things. Dawn got irritated over the way Michael insisted on squeezing the toothpaste tube in the middle, rather than from the bottom. She found his manner of arriving home after work, pouring himself a drink and sitting in front of the television both inconsiderate and selfish. Michael felt frustrated by Dawn's constant nagging about DIY jobs around the house and her refusal to let him relax when he wanted.

TOGETHER BUT SOMETHING MISSING

We discussed the stage of the relationship they were experiencing – commonly known as the misery stage. This is characterised by both people having slipped into 'roles', which are unconscious behaviours that contribute to a sense of deadness and disillusionment. When we dug underneath the surface debris we discovered that both Michael and Dawn were holding on to memories of past lovers in the form of letters, photographs and fantasies about how things could have been. This is not an intelligent thing to do.

When I challenged them about their stored memories they were initially reluctant to recognise the impact that these had. Michael said it was important to him that he kept his mementos because they gave him a sense of value. The trouble is that by letting your self-worth be influenced by old lovers you never discover your true worth today. You project a sense of unworthiness on to your current relationship and hold it responsible for any lack of fulfilment. Dawn claimed that reminding herself of her past relationships made her feel that she wasn't missing out in her life now. She saw several of her friends having affairs due to the unhappiness they were experiencing, and believed that holding on to past relationships prevented her from doing that. I pointed out that whether you're having an actual affair or you're attached to a memory you make yourself unavailable to the potential of your primary relationship.

Cutting the ties that bind you to past lovers is essential for a healthy relationship. It is your willingness to let go that enables this to happen. I had Michael and Dawn undertake a powerful process together. In one session I requested that they bring their old mementos to share with each other. They both felt embarrassed at this prospect but their commitment to moving on was greater than their desire to stay stuck. Michael spoke first and shared with Dawn his history of old lovers. The key during this process was his desire to move on. If he had done it to reinforce the past and undermine the relationship it would not have worked. Dawn followed suit and upon completion we performed a ceremony, burning the old letters and photographs. They both experienced a sense of release as they watched them burn. This enabled them to renew their choice to be loving and intimate together.

What do past lovers represent to you? Do they symbolise passion and lust, a yearning for wild abandonment, or a sense of freedom and excitement? If so, you are caught up in a fantasy that prevents you from giving yourself fully to your relationship now. You will never have a clear perception of your present relationship as long as you hold on to these images.

You do not need to go through the process that Michael and Dawn experienced to say goodbye to past lovers, although having the courage to face these scenarios together is a powerful expression of your commitment. Other forms include:

◈ Burning old letters and photographs yourself.
◈ Writing letters to past lovers in which you communicate any unexpressed thoughts and feelings, which you also burn or throw away – (these letters are purely for the purpose of letting go of old attachment).
◈ Imagining yourself free and released from past connections.
◈ Saying 'no' when fantasies of past lovers come into your mind.

Letting go of the BIG fears

The two greatest fears in relationships are – *the fear of rejection* and *the fear of intimacy*. It is ironic that although they are direct opposites they function alongside each other, creating havoc within a relationship. The most important thing to understand about fear is that *fear is rooted in the past*. You fear rejection because you have felt hurt and abandoned in the past. You fear intimacy because you have felt trapped and emotionally suffocated in the past. The type of fear I am talking about waits backstage, making its presence known at the first available cue. It interprets a relationship through the lens of its particular preference, rejection or intimacy, and becomes the lead character with very little prompting. The trouble with this type of fear is that it prevents you from seeing the truth about a relationship because it colours your perception.

Tracing the origins of fear can take you back to the beginnings of your life. In working with countless people I have observed certain patterns emerging linked to fear. The fear of rejection can stem from feeling unwanted by your parents, for example; maybe they were unmarried and not planning pregnancy, or perhaps they wanted a child of the opposite sex. It is common for people to feel rejected on their first day of school; they want to be liked and popular and yet don't feel it. If they didn't fit in with their peer group they might have felt rejected. The fear of intimacy can also be traced to early experiences in life; maybe a parent was overbearing in their love and attention, or was emotionally distant. If a child experiences the pain of divorce he/she might be afraid to become intimate in the future. These are all understandable scenarios which, if unresolved, are detrimental to our relationships today.

Both these fears are also linked to low self-esteem. The rejection storyline is: I'm unworthy of attracting a loving partner; I therefore seek people who are unsuitable, which reconfirms my lack of self-worth. The intimacy storyline is: as soon as I start getting too intimate with someone I reject them because they can't be worth much if they are interested in me. This is known as *Impostor Syndrome*: the fear that you are about to be unmasked as a fraud. You believe that you do not deserve to have what you want, or, if you do get it, you believe that you must have tricked someone into thinking that you are something you are not.

I used to suffer from both the fear of rejection and intimacy. I did not believe that I was attractive and therefore anticipated rejection every step of the way in the dating game. I found that the women I was attracted to weren't attracted to me, and that the women I wasn't attracted to were attracted to me! It was a confusing time.

The turning point came when I faced these fears head on. I was single and looking at another weekend without any relationship hopes. On the advice of a friend I decided to shut myself away in my home, draw the curtains, take the phone off the hook and experience the full wrath of the demons. During the next 48 hours I watched my self-doubt, feelings of guilt and insecurity about relationships. I confronted my loneliness and came out the other side, still alive. I re-entered the world with a new outlook. I no longer felt dominated by my fears. I held a new perspective. I no longer took relationships personally. I was able to begin to date with ease, which was an extraordinary experience. The key to my new-found success was a quality of detachment that I brought to relationships. Having let go of my main fears, I was freed to be myself.

When you are totally present in a relationship everything is clear and manageable. You no longer react from past references but are proactive to what is here and now. Giving up the fear of rejection and intimacy liberates you to step out of your comfort zone and shine. Remember this – a fear is often *False Evidence Appearing Real*. What you fear might not be the truth. When I faced my fears I learnt that they were not real. I was able to re-interpret them and let them go. To stay afraid keeps you stuck. You never go beyond your fears because the nature of fear is that it stops you in your tracks.

The following three steps help you to leave your fear in the past:

1. Have the courage to face your fear. Running from it will keep you afraid.
2. Have the strength to feel your fear. Blocking fear keeps it alive.
3. Take the risk of following your dreams. Your relationships will transform as you let go of your fears.

The past is over. It is yesterday's story. Today is a clean page waiting for you to make new choices. The next chapter shows you how to make intelligent choices for your relationship fulfilment.

2

Know What You Want to say 'YES' to

THE PRINCIPLE OF CHOICE

When I ask people what they want in relationships, the majority respond by telling me what they don't want. Popular answers include: 'I don't want to lose my independence', 'I don't want the emotional angst that can accompany a relationship', 'I don't want the commitment or responsibility', or 'I don't want the heartbreak if it ends'. The trouble with this type of thinking is that by focusing your attention on what you don't want instead of what you do, it prevents you from having the relationships that you truly want.

The major obstacle to knowing what you want to say 'yes' to is your past. As we have discovered in the last chapter, anything unresolved from your past colours your perception, clouds your thinking and impacts on your behaviour and choices in detrimental ways. The extent to which you are willing to let your past be over is the extent to which you are willing to have what you want now.

Knowing what you want to say 'yes' to is the beginning of creating what you want. It is a commitment to valuing and prioritising what is important to you in relationships and requires courage and flexibility to put it into practice. Some of the key ingredients in knowing what you want to say 'yes' to include:

◆ Daring to love someone regardless of the outcome of the relationship.

◆ Holding your nerve when the going gets tough.
◆ Connecting with your partner when you want to pull away.
◆ Being prepared to do whatever it takes.
◆ Rising to the challenge of balancing work and time together.
◆ Getting excited about the rollercoaster of the ride.
◆ Being willing to grow together.
◆ Communicating when you want to shut down.
◆ Going past your own past self-doubt, fears and unworthiness.
◆ Letting good things happen.
◆ Keeping your heart open and loving fully.

Naturally, it's a big challenge to say a wholehearted 'yes' in the difficult moments. It's easy to say 'yes' when love is in the air, romance is flourishing and everything is going your way. When the love appears to have been extinguished, your partner seems to be a noose around your neck and everything feels as though it were conspiring against you, it is tempting to quit. I have witnessed relationships on the edge of breaking up transformed by one person's willingness to go beyond their past habits and take a stand for something new.

The opening for this transformation lies in the principle of choice. The most profound illustration that I have discovered of the power of choice is in the work of Viktor Frankl. An Austrian psychiatrist and a Jew, Frankl was a survivor of the horrors of the concentration camps in Nazi Germany. He was also a determinist raised in the tradition of Freudian psychology which, simply put, claims that you are a product of your past conditioning, particularly whatever happens to you as a child, and that basically, you can't do much about it.

From his experiences in the death camps, Frankl began to become aware of the phenomenon of choice. He recognised that his captors could control his entire environment, they could do what they wanted to his body, but through his powers of observation he saw that he could decide within himself how all of this was going to affect him. Between the stimulus of what happened to him and his response to it was a gap, within which he could *choose* his response. This ability to choose was what he later called 'the last of the human freedoms' – *our ability to choose our response in any given situation, to choose our own way.*

To apply this to your relationships means that whatever the current stimulus coming at you, it is up to you how you respond to it. For example, if your husband spends the majority of his time at work and at the pub, the choices you make in response to the situation will determine the outcome. To choose to nag him, get angry with him or lose interest in him will probably fuel his behaviour even more. To make new choices such as understanding his position, discussing it honestly and being willing to see it differently will create new consequences.

A further aspect of the principle of choice is recognising that you are responsible for your own life. Taking ownership of that responsibility means that you relate to your partner in conscious and creative ways, instead of reacting to them based on past experience. Asking yourself the following questions shows you how strong your commitment is to taking responsibility:

◆ How willing are you to be responsible for your relationship working?
◆ How committed are you to your relationship working?
◆ Do you plan to participate actively in your relationship?
◆ How willing are you to be honest and authentic in your relationship?

In theory, you may answer that you are willing to be responsible, fully committed, participate actively and be honest and authentic. When we feel upset or victimised it is easy to let these intentions slip. Thankfully, we have the gift of being able to choose and choose again if we do fail. This chapter guides you in making intelligent choices in order to have what you really want.

Saying YES to YOU

The most important relationship you have is with yourself. All other relationships follow from this one. Therefore, until you are able wholeheartedly to say 'yes' to yourself, *you will not let anyone else say 'yes' to you – and get away with it!* Ask yourself: how reasonable is it to expect someone to love you more than you love yourself? If someone did, ultimately you would find it unacceptable because it would not match your self-concept.

I was certainly caught in this trap. I used to struggle to feel good about myself. I placed my self-worth in areas such as my work and relationships, and if they didn't work out in the way that I planned, I would stop saying 'yes' to myself. In my days as a single man, a good proportion of my time was taken up with looking for the 'right' person. I believed that if I could meet Miss 'Right' it would make me feel okay about myself – at which point I could say 'yes' to myself. During this period I took numerous trips down the 'wrong lane'. I was a grade A student in knowing everything that was 'wrong' with me, however I failed miserably at knowing what was 'right'!

In all my work with people I have never met anyone who has truly overestimated how wonderful they are. It is a favourite condition to play ourselves down, look for the faults and undermine our attractiveness. We are very practised at saying 'yes, but' about ourselves and far less accustomed to just saying 'yes'.

To say 'yes, but' is the result of forgetting who you really are. You create a story about yourself based on your interpretation of what happens in your life. Some of the most common stories include:

- I would love myself but I haven't achieved enough.
- I would be kind to myself but I don't deserve it.
- I would let someone love me but I'm not worthy.
- I would be intimate but I can't handle it.
- I would relax and enjoy life but I haven't worked hard enough.

These are all stories based on self-condemnation, putting yourself down and undervaluing your self-worth. The trouble with this type of thinking is that there is never a finishing line that enables you to eliminate the 'but.' I have known high achievers who are still waiting to love themselves. I have known people who work long hours who cannot let themselves relax. I have known kind and generous people who can't be compassionate with themselves.

Being able to identify your story helps you to make new choices about yourself. Seeing it for what it is, a story that you have written, that you no longer believe in, means that you can let it go. In order to discover your story ask yourself, '*my problem in life is . . .*' Spend several minutes writing down your major complaints, the ways in which you suffer and what's not working for you. Then ask your partner or a trusting friend to listen as you read it aloud over and over again, with both of you having the commitment to hear it as a story. As you continue to read your identification with it will change. You might experience feelings of boredom, irritation and frustration. This is completely natural. However, there will be a turning point that comes about through your willingness to see yourself in a new light, and to give up your story.

One of the great gifts that a relationship offers is that it reflects back to you how you see yourself. I believe that this is why relationships become somewhat intense. It's comparable to looking in a mirror 24 hours a day and not always liking what you see. To have your story reflected back to you makes it tempting to hold your partner responsible for any unhappiness. If you catch yourself doing this make a point of thanking them for providing an opportunity to let go of your story. This means that you are taking responsibility for your experience of the relationship and no longer blaming them. It also frees you to see who your partner really is instead of projecting your own story on to them.

Another important element of being able to say 'yes' to you is the choice of *self-acceptance*. Ultimately whoever you are with, whatever you achieve and however hard you work, it will never help you to say yes to yourself fully unless you practise self-acceptance. Self-acceptance is a magical powder which, when sprinkled in the smallest amounts, goes to correct your perception of yourself. To accept yourself is the choice to take a stand against the type of judgements that keep you stuck in a box of self-doubt.

I once counselled a client whose life had been transformed by self-acceptance. A self-made millionaire, Bill had worked himself almost to his death. For the previous fifteen years he had pushed himself to achieve his ambitions. He then discovered a potentially malignant lump above his throat. This crisis was to turn around his priorities. He began to look at his relationship with himself, his family and friends. He realised that despite his worldly success he was not at peace within himself. He revealed that there had been an inner voice that constantly told him he wasn't good enough, he messed things up, he could never be happy, he was not grateful enough, and that he was doing things wrong. No amount of trying to convince himself otherwise had worked.

When I introduced the idea of self-acceptance he winced visibly. In his mind it meant resignation. I explained that self-acceptance is choosing to extend love to yourself, whereas resignation is passively giving up. He agreed to practise accepting himself. As he worked on developing this ability he noticed that his inner critical voice quietened. Although it often produced the same dialogue, the intensity lessened. Eventually he discovered a peace that had been his life's search. He no longer had to wait to enjoy his own company.

It is valuable to check on a daily basis how accepting you are of yourself. Your level of self-acceptance directly relates to your self-esteem, which in turn corresponds to how much love you can handle. To value yourself and enjoy self-confidence enables you to have what you want in relationships.

A useful exercise is to take a moment to close your eyes and ask: *on a scale of 0–100% how much do I truly accept myself?* (0 is not at all, 100 is total) Once you have the figure in your mind imagine on your next in-breath increasing your self-acceptance by one point on the scale. With each in-breath keep moving up the scale until you reach 100%. Doing this on a regular basis renews your commitment to self-acceptance.

The ability to say yes wholeheartedly to you provides the

foundation from which you can choose to let go of the following relationship dynamics that are major obstacles to enjoying love and intimacy.

The choice to go beyond neediness

I watched some good friends move in together recently. They had both been single for some time so it was a big change for them to adapt to living under the same roof. One night they invited me over for dinner. It was an enjoyable evening but Adrian was not being his normal self. In between courses I asked him what was on his mind. He said he had an uneasy feeling that he needed Sam but was afraid to tell her in case she felt burdened. He had been tiptoeing around her for days trying to summon the courage to say it.

I asked Adrian how he would feel if she told him the same thing. He said that he would welcome it with the understanding that we do need other people in order to have fulfilled lives. That was the cue he required. He went next door into the kitchen and gently told Sam that he needed her. She laughed and said that she wondered what had been on his mind and that she needed him too.

We all have needs that can only be met in relationships. To be loved, respected, understood and appreciated are some of the basic needs vital to our health and happiness. However it is important that we make a distinction between need and neediness. Neediness is at the root of co-dependency, which is an inappropriate reliance on another, resulting in the inability to maintain and nurture successful relationships with others and ourselves.

There are two distinct patterns of neediness: compliance or playing the martyr, sacrificing yourself in relation to others; and control or dominating and manipulating others. The following questionnaires will help you to identify if you tend to be more compliant or controlling in your relationships. Answer each question *Always, Usually, Sometimes,* or *Never* (and smile as you go!)

Compliance in relationships

♦ Do you assume responsibility for other people's feelings and behaviour?

♦ Do you feel guilty about other people's feelings and behaviour?

♦ Do you have difficulty in identifying what you are feeling?

♦ Do you have difficulty expressing feelings?

♦ Do you worry how others may respond to your feelings, opinions and behaviours?

♦ Do you value the opinions and feelings of others more than your own?

♦ Do you have difficulty making decisions?

♦ Are you afraid of being hurt and/or rejected?

♦ Do you put other people's needs and desires before your own?

♦ Are you embarrassed to receive recognition, praise and gifts?

♦ Do you judge everything you think, say or do, as 'not good enough'?

♦ Are you a perfectionist?

♦ Do you refrain from asking others to meet your needs or desires?

♦ Do you perceive yourself as a loveable and worthwhile person?

♦ Do you compromise your own values and integrity to avoid rejection or others' anger?

Control in relationships

♦ Do you strive to keep your independence?

♦ Do you get angry and blame others when you don't get your needs met?

♦ Do you dominate others by making them fear you?

♦ Are your moods unpredictable?

♦ Do you focus your attention on protecting others?

♦ Do you believe most people are incapable of taking care of themselves?

♦ Do you keep a score of 'good deeds and favours', becoming hurt when they are not repaid?

- Are you very skilled at guessing how other people are feeling?
- Do you become resentful when others will not let you help them?
- Do you feel good about yourself only when you are helping others?
- Do you freely offer others advice and directions without being asked?
- Do you constantly put aside your own interests and concerns in order to do what others want?
- Do you ask for help and nurturing only when you are ill and then reluctantly?
- Do you use sex to gain approval and acceptance?
- Do you attempt to convince others of how they 'truly' think and 'should' feel?
- Do you perceive yourself as completely unselfish and dedicated to the well-being of others?

It is important not to judge yourself for noticing these patterns. I have yet to meet a human being who does not behave in at least one of these ways. As you raise your personal awareness, you can choose new responses to situations that you might have previously reacted to in either a compliant or controlling manner.

I have certainly exhibited both types of behaviour! In my early relationships I tended to be compliant. I was afraid of being hurt and/or rejected so I compromised myself to the extent of sometimes losing my identity. The irony was that it never helped a relationship because behaving in a compliant way is not attractive. In one particular relationship I spent hours in the pub to avoid getting rejected. Given that I disliked drinking excessive amounts and smoke-filled environments, it was a major sacrifice (and expensive!). Eventually my partner ended the relationship, complaining that I was boring. Since compliancy leads to a loss of your spontaneous self it was not surprising that I was not great company.

On the rebound I then turned my attention to becoming

controlling. I strove to keep my independence at all costs, refusing to commit and getting angry if things weren't going my way. In one relationship I mentally kept a scorecard for the number of favours I performed and was irritated if my partner disagreed with my opinion. I justified my behaviour by believing that I was helping her for the better and I would dominate by threatening to leave.

What you find in a relationship often is that one person leans towards being the 'control freak', and the other acts out the martyr role. The two positions complement each other like a hand in a well-fitting glove, which mean that people can remain stuck in the same roles for many years.

I had a client called Maureen, who came to see me at the end of a painful marriage. She had acted in a compliant manner throughout the relationship. She had sacrificed her career aspirations, been at her husband's beck and call and felt destroyed emotionally and mentally. Her husband exhibited controlling behaviour in an extreme way. He worked all hours, refused to make plans together, socialised with his male friends and kept her on a tight leash. Any attempts Maureen made to try and confront the situation were met with an angry denial that anything was wrong. She was consumed with guilt about ending the relationship because she felt responsible for his feelings.

In order to have the courage to separate Maureen had to be reminded about the reality of her marriage and the treatment that she had received. She could be objective about it only when I asked her to step out of the situation and imagine that it was happening to somebody else. During those periods she could regain her strength and determination to follow through her decision.

If you have been compliant for a long period of time there is a tendency to pretend that everything is okay, in order to look good to others. This pattern prevents you from receiving the support you require to give up being compliant. It takes fearlessness and the encouragement of caring people to help you let it go.

Bob was a client who displayed the chronic need to control. He stated that he was comfortable only as an independent person who called the shots. The trouble was that he had no intimacy in his life, because you cannot be independent and intimate. Repeatedly he attracted women who claimed that they wanted to be independent but then became disempowered by his dominating behaviour.

It came as a shock to Bob to realise the pattern he was caught in; his pride was dented and he tried to justify it by claiming that women were too needy. Over a period of several months he was able to wean himself off the need to control by learning to express his feelings rather than intellectualising them, which is a common trait in an independent person. He found it challenging because his identity had been so dependent on controlling situations. But his commitment to going beyond this form of neediness led him to create honest and healthy relationships.

Becoming aware of these patterns is a crucial step to freeing yourself from them. Ask yourself: *what is the cost involved in continuing to be compliant or controlling?* This gives you leverage if you're tempted to fall back into old habits. Ask for help from supportive friends who will hold you to your commitment to change. Your willingness to make new choices and go beyond the patterns of neediness connects you to the real purpose of a relationship – to love and be loved. It allows you to give fully and unconditionally. The expectations that restrict the potential of a relationship are removed and you open yourself to a new level of intimacy and spontaneity.

Choose to connect

One of the major reasons we exhibit controlling or compliant behaviour is the experience of separation. To believe that we are separate from others and the world is soul-destroying. In a relationship it causes us to feel isolated and alone. It can make us shut down emotionally, withdraw our love, cut off communication and perceive our partner as an enemy and not a friend.

Separation is an illusion. Think about what happens when

someone dies. Although their physical body is no longer here, their presence is alive within you. We are connected by an invisible thread which is at the core of being human. It is insane to think that there are six billion people on the planet, all of whom are separate from each other. The belief in separation is at the root of the epidemic of independence today. We have come to worship it, but it is impossible to be independent and happy. It is a reflection of fear because in order to preserve separation you must defend yourself against others.

The starting point in healing separation is to connect with yourself. As long as you believe that you are separate you search outside yourself for a sense of wholeness and love. This is self-defeating because *you are what you seek*. The happiness, peace and fulfilment that you yearn for are already within. There is nothing missing within you. To believe otherwise is to identify with your story, the interpretation that you have given your life so far, which causes you to stay stuck in the past.

The choice to give up the thought of separation is the decision to let go of fear, defensiveness, competitiveness, envy and attack, which are at the heart of relationship conflict. At a recent Relationship Intelligence Workshop there was a couple called Paul and Marianne who had been married for nearly a year and were on the verge of splitting up. They were arguing continuously, both felt unsupported by the other and their differences seemed insurmountable. I suggested that they look past the drama of the relationship and focus on the dynamic behind it. Being able to spot a dynamic helps you to stop playing it out. When I described the symptoms of separation they realised this was the dynamic which had been driving their communication and behaviour. Being able to identify the source of their broken trust, hurt feelings and painful communication came as a considerable relief. They were able to rebuild the marriage with the benefit of recognising when they were caught in the separation dynamic.

Separation is at the root of deadness. If you have ever experienced the vitality and juice going out of your relationship it is primarily due to separation. Holding on to the belief in separation puts you in conflict with your partner and drains the relationship of its aliveness. Conflict is hard work. It is exhausting to hold on to an antagonistic position out of pride. It means that you have to put the shutters up over your heart, which, once closed, remove you from the presence of love, compassion and joy.

Once you've hit separation the challenge is to reconnect. Remember that as long as you hold on to separation you will never find what you are looking for. A helpful choice that you can make is to detach from it. In Buddhism this is called the practice of mindfulness, which means simply being aware of and living in this present moment. To be mindful of separation is to observe it, as if you were watching a movie on the screen of your mind. This brings about detachment, which enables you to reclaim objectivity. Sometimes people confuse detachment and denial. Denial is when you perform 'ostrich thinking', or burying your head in the sand and pretending nothing is happening. Detachment is being honest about your experience of separation, but not making it real.

The next time you catch yourself feeling separate take a moment to: Identify it, and take responsibility for your experience of separation. Imagine standing back from it and viewing it like a movie. Silently say to yourself 'separation, separation, separation'. Watch it passing by. Bring your attention to the present moment. Choose to connect.

The choice to connect utilises your power to go beyond the past. To bring this into your relationship frees you from the grip of fear that keeps you separate. Walls of defiance collapse, positions of pride soften and the need to be righteous dissipates. This provides an opening that enables you to connect with and experience your unity. I suggest reading the following meditation when you find separation dominating your relationship:

I open myself to the possibility of true connection.

I have felt blocked, shut down and withheld. I acknowledge that this does not help my relationship and leaves me feeling isolated, disillusioned and separate.

I notice my stubbornness, impatience and desire to be 'right'. These do not support me. They are based on fear and lack, and are a futile attempt to create a relationship.

I choose another way. I surrender and lay down my old behaviour, beliefs and perceptions.

Where I have been blind I open myself to the light. Where I have been weak I am reminded of my strength. Where I have been confused I let clarity enter.

I open my heart to this person now.

I surrender to the love that is available to us.

I welcome the joy that is always present.

I let go of any limitations that I have placed between myself and the experience of harmony in my relationship.

Let me love as I have not loved.

Let me understand as I have not understood, and see what I have not seen so that we might both be freed from the prison of separation.

The process of reconnection comes not from improving our 'people skills' but from developing our 'soul skills'. The key is to move beyond the normal reality of thought and behaviour to the silent rhythms that only the spirit perceives. In this way you access dimensions of a relationship which have previously been hidden to you. We are not bound by the physical level of a relationship, unless we choose to be. There is a realm of freedom and joy that transcends the expectations and conditions we have created. Let us use the intelligence of love to heal the conflict and pain of separation.

Great expectations

What do you expect from a relationship? What are the rules that you have made up? What are the roles that should be played? Asking yourself these questions can be uncomfortable, yet unless you face them honestly it's possible to let expectations destroy your relationships. An expectation is an opinion that something 'should be' a certain way. It is the belief that you should get what you want, in your own way. You wait for what you believe is owed to you to be given to you and you get upset if it doesn't appear. For example, when you wake up in the morning and it's raining you get upset because you expect it to be sunny. When you go to the bathroom after a big night out and it's busy, you get upset because you expect it to be empty. When you come home at the end of the day and your partner doesn't listen to you, you get upset because you expect to be listened to.

The trouble with living in a world of expectations is that holding fixed, rigid positions creates no room for flexibility. Without flexibility and the willingness to see things differently, to shift your perception and to change your outlook, you can easily be upset. It prevents you from creating future possibilities that transform your current experience of life and relationships.

Jill had expected so much out of her marriage. She had so many dreams. None of them had come true. She felt that she had been tricked, betrayed and let down. Her home and marriage – the place and person that should have been warm, nurturing, a comfort and a haven of peace – had become a trap. She kept telling herself that it would get better. After all, she believed that the problems were her husband's fault. When he stopped working so hard, when he gave her more attention, when he made their marriage a priority, things would get better.

Jill came to see me at this moment of crisis. As a starting point I asked her to disclose what her expectations had been in the relationship. She had expected that they would be best friends but now they hardly spoke to each other, and if they did it was through clenched teeth. She had expected to share the daily chores but now they were left to her. She had expected to enjoy relaxing holidays but now they spent them in tense silence pretending to have a good time. She had expected to have children but now they never had sex let alone discussed the possibility of children.

As Jill continued talking she began to see how past conditioning had created her expectations. She could hear her mother talking, and she cringed. She had tried so hard to do it differently from the role models she saw around her whilst growing up. Slowly she began to see that maybe it wasn't all her husband's 'fault' but that due to her expectations she had dug a hole for the relationship.

Our expectations place a frame around a relationship and create a limiting concept. They are formed out of fear and lead to rules being made and roles being played. Whenever you are playing a role you are not being your authentic self. Therefore your partner does not get the person they originally chose to be with, but a carbon copy under the influence of an expectation. To suffer from 'role decay' kills a relationship because it takes away the spontaneity and self-expression that help it to be fulfilled.

A rule is an unspoken agreement governing a relationship. One of the primary rules formed by expectations is to maintain the status quo. It states: 'if you meet my expectations and I meet yours, we will live happily ever after'. This is all very well until the moment when they are not met, which is often when a relationship breaks down. We feel betrayed and let down yet all that has happened is that our expectations are unfulfilled.

Carl and Sue came to see me claiming that their primary source of unhappiness lay in their expectations of their relationship. They were caught in stereotypical roles which caused both of them distress. He expected her to cater to his every need and she expected him to provide the security and lifestyle she wanted. By bringing this into the open, they chose to dissolve their expectations and commit to a path that would allow their relationship to grow.

Carl took responsibility for meeting his own needs. He started to play sport regularly, which gave balance to his working life. He took an interest in cooking, learning simple but delicious recipes that added a new dimension to their home life. Sue put more energy into her work. She focused on her creativity, enabling her to experience greater fulfilment and eventually to earn more money. This enabled her to move away from her dependency on Carl and to recognise that the source of her security lay within herself.

The way to give up expectations is simply to tell the truth about them. They are another aspect of your story which you can rewrite, opening the door to making new choices. For example, you can choose to be fully present to your partner and give up living in the past. You can choose to be excited about your relationship and not allow it to be routine. You can choose to be intimate and stop being busy and distracted. Giving up expectations, roles and rules enables creative growth and movement and is a powerful expression of saying yes to enjoying a fulfilled relationship.

Shared winnings!

Susan was having the time of her life. She had just received a promotion at work and all was going well. Simon, her partner, felt jealous. Although he appeared to celebrate her good fortune, he experienced pangs of envy and became short-tempered. He started arguments over nothing in particular. Upon discussion he realised that he felt insecure about her success. He perceived himself as rejected as she was now getting on with her life. When they first got together he had provided the emotional and financial support that had enabled her to create the life she wanted. Now that she was living it he feared he no longer had a part to play.

It is a common dilemma that when one person thrives their partner may feel threatened. On the whole, we tend to be more comfortable with limited success because it maintains the status quo. We can greet each other with doom and gloom and share the misery of the day rather than rocking the boat with good news. In order for a relationship to develop it is essential for both people to genuinely celebrate each other's happiness and success. It takes a measure of internal security not to feel threatened by your partner's growth.

The approach required to share each other's happiness is to think win/win. There is an understanding that when you win or receive what you want, your partner wins too, and that when they win, you win. To employ win/win thinking requires a flexible and creative mind. It is a belief in a better way. It opens doors to new choices, powerful communication, deeper understanding and shared success.

Past conditioning usually influences us to think win/lose, or if one person wins, others lose. This is most notable in sport and exists in many other types of situations. The business world is rife with competition and win/lose thinking. Politics is heavily weighted toward win/lose thinking and so are relationships. Win/lose thinking is based on a scarcity paradigm, dominated by a belief that there is not enough of anything to go around. The result is that it creates competition, rivalry and vengeful behaviour.

At one of my workshops Tom and Helen talked about their relationship, which was dominated by win/lose thinking. It was highlighted over the decision whether or not to have children. Helen was in her early thirties, worked full-time as a teacher and felt ready to have a child. Tom was a similar age and also worked full-time, but did not want to have children yet. Whenever they raised the subject it ended in conflict, with Helen feeling unheard and Tom feeling pressured. I encouraged them to reflect on their individual attitudes. Helen discovered that she feared rejection and perceived Tom's reluctance as a personal attack. He believed that a child would restrict his career options as well as taking away from the quality of their relationship. He felt that they had enough responsibilities and insufficient quality time together as it was.

I then asked them to apply win/win thinking to their predicament. Initially they both resisted the idea because they wanted to be 'right'. Realising that this was not a way forward, they agreed to listen to each other without letting their own interpretations take over. This meant that their individual views could be heard in an unthreatening way, which was a win/win situation. It created space for mutual understanding, bringing them closer together, from which position they could discuss future possibilities. Helen discovered that by feeling heard, her fear of rejection subsided. Tom found that he started to see the gifts that a child would bring, which lightened his perception of it. They agreed to strengthen their commitment to think win/win and found that it provided a valuable compass to follow for approaching life and making decisions.

Win/win thinking is an intelligent choice. It creates opportunities and moves you away from a victim mentality, when you perceive yourself as having no choice in a situation and feel powerless and compelled to compromise your values. You can use it as a foundation for making the simplest to the most complex decisions. For example, if you are going for an evening out and you want to see a film whilst your partner wants to have dinner, thinking win/win means that you look for a solution to meet both your needs. You might decide that tonight you go to the movies and next time you go for dinner, or you could agree to do something completely different. The key is that you make an agreement that you both feel good about.

A more challenging situation is getting the balance right between your relationship and work. To think win/win causes you to put aside your everyday thoughts, jettison your judgements, put down your fears and make yourself available to higher wisdom. You might choose to express your positions on where you stand regarding the relationship and work, acknowledging any difficulty that you experience. You may decide to look at options until you reach an agreement that meets both of your needs. This could include scheduling sacred time together that is untouched no matter how pressing other issues appear, getting highly organised on the home front to ensure that you don't waste precious time together, and increasing your effectiveness at work in order to accomplish more in less time. To be committed to win/win creates an excitement in your relationship, deepening trust and building cooperation.

A further option of win/win thinking is to agree to disagree. In other words if there is no apparent solution, then agreeing to disagree is the appropriate step to take. This creates an environment in which you can value each other's differences, preventing you from letting righteousness take over. The notion that you should agree on everything to have a good relationship is a myth. It's healthy to be able to agree to disagree and not to take it personally.

Your commitment to win/win thinking is a choice to see the abundance that is made possible from being in a relationship. As Bob Mandel once wrote, 'Two hearts are better than one'. Celebrating this truth draws out the very best of being together.

Letting yourself receive

The amount of love, happiness and intimacy that you enjoy in a relationship is directly linked to your ability to receive it. To receive is to say 'yes' to the possibility of creating an extra-ordinary relationship which is fun, dynamic and alive. It is to let in the love that your partner has to give. In order to have a fulfilled relationship both people must learn to be good receivers, otherwise an imbalance in giving and receiving occurs, which deprives you of the joy of mutual exchange.

I used to find it difficult to receive because I believed that I wasn't worthy of receiving good things, and that if I did, I was beholden to the giver. Dissecting this dynamic made me realise that it was my way of trying to control a relationship. By resisting receiving I could stay separate without fully letting in their love. My habit was to push love away and then to complain that I never received as much as I gave. I played the role of martyr and felt sorry for myself. Obviously there was a high price to pay in carrying on this way. It deprived me of intimacy, love and fun. Confronting this pattern provided the springboard to make changes for the better. I decided to start letting myself receive in order to achieve a healthy balance between giving and receiving.

How do you prevent yourself from receiving? Do you believe that you haven't worked hard enough or suffered enough to receive? Do you deflect compliments because it's uncomfortable to receive? Do you postpone receiving whilst you 'wait' for your life to start?

Receiving is the art of keeping your heart open, being defence-less and trusting others. To block receiving is to believe that you have to sacrifice yourself and your life. It has its roots in low self-esteem, which causes you to feel unworthy. Tell-tale signs that you are suffering from a low receiving threshold include: when people give to you, you wait for the catch, the hidden agenda, or the not-so-happy ending. You ask yourself what have you done to deserve this, and tell yourself that they can't be much themselves if they want to give to you.

Letting yourself receive means giving up the impression that you are undeserving or not good enough. It requires you to value yourself highly and become comfortable with letting good things happen. We have been led to believe that receiving is selfish and self-centred. However, think about what happens when you stop yourself from receiving. You become resentful, hold grudges, burn out, and ultimately have less to give to others.

It is impossible for your relationship to grow and blossom unless you are willing to receive. In the absence of receiving you get stuck in muddy ground because you have closed the door to moving forward. Expectations creep in, control dominates, demands mount up and struggle is the name of the game. You play the role of victim, holding your partner responsible for your stagnation when the solution is for you to say 'yes' to receiving again.

When you are a child you receive without questioning. Your first nine months are spent receiving five-star womb service that is good preparation for your future. When you enter the world, unless you are unwanted, you are received with love and joy. This continues until outside conditioning creeps in, warping your understanding of receiving. You hear messages such as 'there will be tears before bedtime', 'no pain, no gain', and 'all good things come to an end'. Disillusionment can set in and you may become resigned to living half-heartedly.

Your willingness to receive again is the first step to resolving this dilemma. Ask yourself: *'What do I want to receive more of in my relationship?'* Is it love, joy, fun, intimacy, compassion? What stops you from being a better receiver? Are you afraid, do you feel unworthy, do you believe it's selfish? Notice your response, and be willing to let these obstacles go. You can have whatever you want if you are willing to receive it.

The second step is to truly let yourself receive when your partner gives to you. If you are paid a compliment, say 'thank you', instead of deflecting it with a well-worn excuse. If you are given a gift receive it unconditionally. The joy of receiving is that it is a blessing for the giver. It is disheartening when you want to genuinely give to someone and they push it away.

It is your responsibility to receive in a relationship. Each day choose to be a great receiver. Learn to say 'yes' when your partner gives you love and support. The generosity of receiving lets you see who they really are, and allows you both to thrive and live fully.

3

Now is New!

THE PRINCIPLE OF TRANSFORMATION

Bob and Linda have been together for over 24 years. You might think that due to familiarity their love could have died, but to spend time with them is comparable to being in the presence of new lovers. They are as passionate now about each other as when they first met. When I asked them the secret of their happiness they said something that has stayed close to my heart: *'In every moment we have a choice to let the flame of love burn bright, or to let it fade without a trace.'*

We can transform a relationship, no matter how difficult it may have been, through our willingness to leave yesterday behind and open to a new start today. We don't have to understand the process of transformation at a rational level, just as we cannot logically explain the metamorphosis of a caterpillar into a beautiful butterfly. It is a gift of nature which we can experience in a relationship.

The benefit of transformation is that you can create a relationship anew without having to end it or suffer needlessly. It can also make the day-to-day experience of being in partnership an exciting adventure. Your ability to recognise unhelpful habits, such as struggle, guilt, helplessness, competitiveness and judgement, and to confront the impact that they have on your life, creates a space out of which new possibilities emerge. This can save years of grief, as it is possible to stay in a relationship with a list of complaints or to leave and re-experience the same difficulties in the next one. It's like the movie *Groundhog Day*, where every day is like yesterday. You get stuck in a rut, while the safety and familiarity that the past provides takes over and prevents you from moving forward.

Sometimes when you are caught in an old habit you cannot conceive of a solution. The problem appears so real that you opt for resignation and cynicism. Although this is understandable it is not a helpful choice to make. Being aware of the power of transformation means that a shift can occur either in your thinking, emotions or action, which has a positive effect on yourself and your life.

As you read on, adopt a beginner's mind approach. Put aside your past opinions and interpretations. Every new moment is an opportunity for growth, evolution and a change of heart that can transform your relationship forever.

Stop the struggle

Pause for a moment and reflect on how it feels to have a relationship consumed by struggle. What is it like constantly to argue over little things? How does it feel when mountains are made out of molehills? How does it affect you when procrastination rules, indecisiveness takes over, conflict abounds and fun is a forgotten memory? The answer to these questions can be summarised in a single word – miserable!

A relationship dominated by struggle is filled with suffering. It lurches from one obstacle to another until someone leaves, or else it stays in a misery zone. Common statements such as, 'life's a bitch and then you die' are its calling card and its theme song is, 'no pain, no gain!' The relationship is locked into a victim mentality which holds on to its identity of struggle for all it's worth. The source of conflict lies in the beliefs that 'life is a struggle' and 'you have to struggle to survive'. The idea of ease and effortless accomplishment appear too threatening to handle, so struggle continues.

The type of struggle I am referring to is different from putting effort into a relationship. Often when people are asked, 'what makes a good relationship?' they reply, 'hard work'. I agree that being prepared to work at a relationship is extremely important but, when that work becomes struggle and everything is perceived as an uphill battle, it's time to ring the changes.

Cast your mind back to the beginning of a relationship. It is a wonderful period; a honeymoon time filled with romantic love, excitement, possibility and adventure. Naturally, it's not all a bed of roses. There might be moments of uncertainty caused by a move into the unknown, but they seem to add to the intensity; struggle is not part of the agenda. So what happens? What changes? Familiarity creeps in and with it, old habits. If struggle has been a pattern for you in the past, you will tend to recreate it until you become aware of it and make the decision to stop.

This form of therapy is known as Stop It Therapy, and it involves the commitment to stop doing what doesn't work and to start doing what does! Struggle doesn't work. No matter how much struggle you bring into a relationship it will not make it any more loving, intimate or enjoyable. To start focusing on what contributes to joy, passion and ease does work, and helps you to re-ignite those qualities.

Veronica and I have had different experiences with struggle. I grew up in an environment that placed a strong emphasis on effort and hard work, which often turned into struggle. Growing up at the Yehudi Menuhin School we had to rise early each morning to start practising our music before breakfast. We often worked through our lunch breaks and had concerts to attend or give in the evening. From the age of eight a normal day for me lasted twelve to fourteen hours. Veronica's background couldn't have been more different. One of a family of eight children in New Zealand, her life was filled with playing in the garden or at the beach. Although her parents had to work extremely hard to raise the family, her overriding memories were of enjoyment and fun.

I carried the habit of struggle into my relationships. I held the belief that unless there was a struggle there was no value to be gained. You can imagine that most of my relationships didn't last long, unless my partner at the time enjoyed struggle! Thankfully now if struggle does arise with Veronica we're able to recognise it fairly quickly. It took me a while to wean myself off the need to have it and I have learnt that having an intelligent relationship is not about struggle. The joy gained from ending struggle is now far greater than the desire to continue it.

Begin to notice the areas that you struggle with in relationships. The most common include: money, communication, time/work and sex. I had a couple attending a workshop whose major complaint was about money. John said that no matter how hard he worked he never seemed to have enough to pay the bills and was constantly in debt. On the other hand Ruth felt abundant financially and was frustrated by his position. I guided John to recall the source of the problem. He remembered that his parents were always short of money and lived in the hope that maybe things would get better. In the meantime they argued and struggled to live within their means. He picked up the message that life is a struggle and resigned himself to that reality.

I asked him to think about the impact that struggling with money had on his relationship. He admitted that it caused painful arguments, broke down trust and encouraged separation. Having confronted the issue John was now able to embrace something new. He warmed to the idea that he could create more money without struggle. Ruth smiled as she saw a new possibility opening together. The starting point for them was to have a transformed relationship with money, which inspired them to stay open to new ideas and opportunities.

Ask yourself: *'The way I struggle in my relationship is . . .'* Identifying and admitting the habit is the first step to letting it go. Then you can take the next step of making a choice to give up struggle, choose peace and let your relationship work in conscious and creative ways.

End guilt

If you are taking a guilt trip in your relationship, beware. It can become a way of life and dominate it to such a degree that it takes away spontaneity, playfulness and pleasure. The experience of guilt gives rise to anxiety, stress and conflict causing breakdowns in communication and in the health of a relationship.

This type of guilt usually stems from our childhood and is a consequence of feeling that we couldn't please our parents or live up to their expectations. Unconsciously we decide that there is something wrong with us, or that we must have done something wrong. Some common examples include: accidentally breaking an object and deciding that you've done something wrong; failing an exam and deciding that you have let your parents down; experiencing your parents' divorce and deciding that it's your fault. By distinguishing the event from the decision about yourself you are able to regain a sense of perspective. Things happen in life, but it's the decisions that you make in response that determine whether you feel guilty or not.

Guilt is the *mafia of the mind*. The mafia works by making you pay them to protect you from them. You tell yourself that as long as I'm feeling guilty it's okay, nobody else can come in and make me feel bad because I already feel so terrible! It is an insurance policy you sell yourself as a form of protection. Unfortunately it never works because the nature of guilt is that it demands punishment. Either you punish yourself through sacrificing your needs and wants or you get your partner to punish you through disapproval or undermining your self-worth. This becomes a vicious circle that rotates around life events, self-judgement, feeling guilty and self-punishment. Guilt is not a solution.

One day I received a phone call from a woman who explained that she was calling on behalf of her husband. He was a senior partner in his company, worked long hours, and had a five-year-old son who didn't sleep. He was on the verge of burn-out. He wanted to come and see me but felt too guilty to take the time to do it. Asking his wife to make an appointment on his behalf was the only way he could make the commitment.

Tim arrived in a flurry of apologies. He apologised for not calling me, for arriving two minutes late and for troubling me with his problems. He described his major issue as not being able to relax and be himself. He felt responsible and obligated to everyone and everything in his life, which felt like a huge burden. He said he wanted to get off the train of life, but he'd spent all his time building up to this point of success and didn't want to let it go.

We started by discussing his past. He revealed how his father either worked or drank in the pub with his friends. His mother suffered a heart condition and there was always concern about her health. His father died when he was fourteen and they were left with very little money so Tim went out to work at the first opportunity. He sacrificed college to support his mother and by the time I saw him had worked for twenty years without a proper break. He said that although he was frustrated and resentful about his past, feelings of guilt about his mother's health and the way she was treated by his father were predominant.

When we looked at the price he was paying for his guilt it was a high one. It cost him his happiness, peace of mind, freedom and self-expression. He couldn't stand up for what he believed at work or communicate effectively. It was spilling into his marriage, causing stress and anxiety. To begin to heal the guilt we did a role-play in which he spoke to his parents. It was an opportunity to express his feelings about his past. He realised that he had blamed himself for his mother's poor health and his father's drinking. In the exercise he declared that he was giving up the guilt; it had sabotaged his life for long enough. He had perceived himself as guilty and was now committed to letting it go.

An important step in ending guilt is to change your mind about yourself. This occurs as a result of forgiving yourself. Forgiveness is the choice to see the light in yourself when you are in the darkness. It is a willingness to see yourself differently, to step beyond your past story and to reclaim your innocence and joy. Picture yourself as a young child, innocent, pure and full of life. This is your essence, who you really are, behind the wall of misperceptions and learned conditioning. Replay this image whenever you are tempted to slip into guilt. It may feel selfish at first, which is part of the reason why we hold on to guilt. In truth, ending guilt is a selfless act because it means that your partner gets to relate to the real you and not to an apologetic shadow.

Helping helplessness

One of the greatest obstacles to happiness in a relationship is the experience of helplessness. To hit helplessness is like being unable to find your way out of a maze; whichever way you turn you reach another dead end. Finally the sheer frustration forces you to give up and you're left feeling disempowered and disillusioned.

Helplessness is governed by two primary beliefs; 'I can't' and 'I don't know'. As soon as we bring either of these into a situation we will experience a block. They cause our brains to shut down and register no response. I once worked with a couple called Matthew and Pam who had hit a wall of helplessness. Their communication was littered with the beliefs 'we can't' and 'don't know' as they attempted to improve their relationship. They had lost the closeness and playfulness that they had once experienced. They said their relationship was a dreary drudge and that they couldn't see a way out. When I asked them why they were still together they responded by saying they didn't know.

I asked them to think about whether the current state of their relationship was similar to their parents' relationships with each other. We started to make progress as Matthew related the story of his parents' marriage. He perceived them arguing constantly but never making any changes. They had slipped into a destructive routine, which subconsciously became his expectation of a relationship. Pam had a slightly different story. Her parents had tried to make the marriage work but eventually separated due to irrevocable differences. She had resigned herself to the belief that however much she put into a relationship it was doomed.

By understanding the influence of their parents' relationships they were able to see their own in a different light. They agreed that whenever one person felt helpless the other would hold open a door of possibility. This strategy enabled them to have faith that a solution would be found. They witnessed the helplessness as an old friend and were no longer dominated by it. To be able to maintain faith when stuck in an old habit is essential, otherwise it can cause you to give up on something of true value.

The next time you hit a wall of helplessness employ 'possibility thinking'. Ask the question: 'what is possible here?' Possibility thinking is a form of lateral thinking, which focuses the mind on looking for alternative options. There has been a lot written about positive thinking and developing a positive mental attitude. Although this is useful and does help, to think positively when you feel helpless is like covering up a wound with a band-aid. It might provide temporary relief but does not heal the condition. Possibility thinking helps you to keep an open mind and to see things differently. Your willingness is the key to experiencing a shift.

It is tempting to fall into a victim mentality when you feel helpless. Blaming your partner or the world might get you a sympathy vote but it will not change the dynamic. Possibility thinking is a way of taking responsibility for your experience. It brings the power back to yourself and reconnects you with your innate creativity.

One of the main ways that I used to experience feeling helpless was in attracting relationships. I had periods of time when I was single yet wanted to be in a relationship. I internalised the sense of helplessness and believed that I wasn't good enough or that there was something wrong with me. It was damaging to my self-esteem and certainly didn't help my cause.

The turning point came when I chose to face the helplessness. I locked myself in my flat for a weekend. I turned off the phone, drew the curtains and decided that instead of trying to fight the feeling or run away from it I was going to experience it fully. Initially, I felt immobilised. I lay on my bed and reflected on how helplessness had played havoc with my perception. I was unable to see things clearly and felt stuck and sorry for myself.

I chose to surrender and accept this experience. I realised that underneath the helplessness was a sense of isolation and separation. I felt alone and on my own. This was the pivotal moment. I could have reinforced this belief and stayed stuck, but thankfully I had the wisdom to employ possibility thinking. I considered the possibility that the sense of separation was based on a false premise and that I could choose to see myself as intrinsically connected to the world around me. This simple act gave me new confidence. I realised how I had turned to relationships to give me a sense of worth and identity and it was time to change the habit. I resumed contact with the world the following Monday morning in a far more peaceful state. I no longer felt helpless. By focusing on my connection with the world I could relax. I began to enjoy a variety of relationships which I would never have attracted if I had stayed stuck in helplessness.

Allowing yourself to surrender to helplessness helps you to let it go. What you resist persists, and the choice to accept it flushes out confusion and brings you back to your innate creativity, which is at the source of transformation.

Love is the best revenge!

Have you ever plotted a complex strategy for getting even with a partner if you've felt hurt or let down? Have you ever withheld your love, shut down communication or been vengeful in your behaviour? If so, welcome to the human being club. The desire for revenge is one of our most powerful emotions, and we can go to considerable lengths to justify it.

The best way to get revenge in a relationship is to keep your heart open and continue loving. Whenever you try and even the score by matching somebody else's behaviour, for example by having an affair, putting someone down, backbiting, or withdrawing love and communication, you lose out. Revenge is not a solution. It might appear to give you temporary satisfaction but that soon passes and you are left licking your wounds.

It takes a great deal of energy to figure out how you are going to get your own back. I have heard people plotting elaborate schemes to try and get the upper hand. It is your life that you are putting on hold whenever you aim to get revenge. Usually the prime motive is established by the belief that you have been wronged. In fact at the heart of most relationship problems are grievances which, if you stay attached to them, keep you stuck in pain. There are certainly situations in which people are hurt, betrayed and wounded in relationships but to try to resolve these by getting revenge is not helpful and prevents transformation.

I worked with a woman called Rebecca who had good reason to wish to get revenge. She had been married for several years and had two young children when she discovered that her husband had been having an affair. She made this discovery after contracting a sexually transmitted disease. When she confronted him initially he denied it but later had to confirm it for medical reasons. He claimed that he had ended the affair and she resumed the marriage only to find out that the woman had become pregnant. His supposed business trips were in fact visits to see her and he subsequently moved in with her. Rebecca was devastated by this and extremely angry. When she first came to see me she was consumed with the desire to get her own back. She found out that he had made some unethical business transactions, which she threatened to use against him. She wanted to turn the children against him and she wanted to nail him financially so that he would pay for his actions. Her entire focus was on getting revenge.

Rebecca pursued this route but soon came unstuck. Every time she made a move he made one, too. He roped her into his past business transactions, he told the children lies about her and refused to pay maintenance. Her health began to suffer and she found it hard to function. Having listened to Rebecca's story I questioned her strategy for recovery. She had the maturity and strength to observe what was happening. Although her primal instinct was for revenge, upon reflection she could see that this was not the way forward.

I asked her to consider the possibility of forgiveness. Since forgiveness moves us back to the present it helps us to undo the pain of the past. I reminded her that forgiveness is to give your love – first to yourself. She wept uncontrollably as she considered forgiving her husband. She noticed that her greatest resistance was a need for righteousness, but the process of talking about it softened the block and she began to see her husband differently. She recognised that he had been trapped in a life of deceit and fear, which prevented him from giving fully in any relationship. This understanding allowed her to move on with her own life. She focused on rebuilding communication with the children, getting a new job and redoing the house. She gave herself time to heal and discovered that by letting go of her need for revenge she experienced greater freedom and peace.

It is a sign of maturity to take responsibility for a relationship grievance instead of looking for revenge. You often hear advice which supports people in getting even and sweeping statements that give rise to stereotypes like 'all men are bastards and can't be trusted', or 'you'd better watch out because women are only interested in money'. These beliefs are fear-based and result in further breakdown of communication and trust.

The way to rebuild a relationship is to let go of grievances and to be willing to see things differently. We all have our side of a story but it is the capacity genuinely to understand somebody else's that causes a return to love. This does not mean that you have to stay in a relationship if it is detrimental to your health and well-being. It does mean that whatever the outcome, your willingness to commit to love and to let the rest go ensures your peace of mind.

It's not a competition

How often do you catch yourself turning your relationship into a competition? 'Who's winning in your relationship?' is a ridiculous question but the goal of winning, to be 'right' about your opinions, beliefs and perceptions, can become more important than qualities such as love, companionship and understanding. When competition takes over power struggles abound, niggling arguments surface and an underlying tension runs the relationship.

The habit of competition usually stems from the experience of it in your family. A common dynamic with siblings is to compete for love and attention from the parents, to be the 'best' child in the family and to 'win' at fights and games with each other. An only child often transfers the competition on to friends or it shows up as the need to be the centre of attention. It is quite natural to be competitive but it becomes a problem when the need to win dominates a relationship, causing damage as a result.

Start to notice when competition begins and follow it through to its conclusion. One couple I worked with were forever arguing over the smallest details. A trip to the supermarket would turn into a race to see who could push the trolley, get their own choice of food and control the whole transaction. Whenever they had to make joint decisions the need to assert an opinion became a greater priority than making the decision. They argued constantly about whose interpretation was 'right' in any situation, which is crazy as an interpretation is simply a matter of opinion. As you can imagine, there was an absence of joy and the partnership was tarnished by such behaviour.

Competition is based on a scarcity mentality or believing that there is not enough to go around, so you must compete to get what you can. People who have a scarcity mentality find it difficult to share love, attention and recognition. They try to dominate conversations and divert attention from others. At the root of a scarcity mentality is fear, which causes them to look for evidence to prove that there is only so much, as though there were only one pie out there. And if someone were to get a big piece of the pie, that they would miss out.

The beauty of true partnership is that you are able to support and co-operate with each other, which takes you into new pastures. Old competitive behaviour falls away as you join together. This togetherness is known as synergy, which recognises that the whole is greater than the sum of its parts. In a relationship it is characterised by co-operation and going for win/win solutions. It allows for a new level of communication as both people unite in the desire for greater understanding and love. The result is an exciting adventure into the unknown, which carries a relationship out of any deadness and into new realms of possibility. A relationship can never be described as dull or boring if there is a real commitment to a synergistic vision.

The essence of synergy is to value differences – to respect them, to build on strengths and to learn and grow together. One of the greatest gifts that you can receive in a relationship is the differences that you both offer. I have certainly benefited greatly from Veronica's different outlook on life and I hope she has by mine.

The key to keeping competition at bay is to recognise it. Take the time to reflect and discuss ways that it prevents you from being synergistic. Maybe you are critical of certain characteristics in your partner and that stops you from appreciating their uniqueness. Perhaps you believe that you know more than they do in a specific area, which inhibits your willingness to consider new options. Synergy requires you to be humble and to recognise your own perceptual limitations. Although you might possess considerable knowledge and skills, to join with another adds new dimensions. To appreciate the rich resources available to you, by connecting with the heart and mind of your partner, is to enjoy the fruits of being together.

Relinquish judgement

When two people fall in love they can do no wrong in each other's eyes. This romantic stage is characterised by large amounts of passion, mutual appreciation, and acceptance. Once the initial wonder passes it is only too easy to slip into negative judgements, which can show up in the form of criticism, put-downs or back-biting comments. You lose your compassion for them and begin to see them in a different light. This type of judgement is extremely painful to handle and if continued destroys the love and companionship previously shared.

It is important to understand that any relationship goes through different stages, which we shall identify later in the principle of change. Although we might yearn for a lifetime of dreams and romance, accepting the natural evolution of a relationship is crucial for its health. The ability to strengthen love at testing times means that ultimately you will enjoy a far deeper and more nourishing relationship. We have had false pictures of relationships painted for us by parents who covered up their own problems and by Hollywood movies creating fictional role models for us to aspire to. The sooner that we accept that our partner is human and is subject to the same flaws as anyone else, the quicker the relationship can be transformed.

Judgement is a form of defensiveness that masks insecurities and lack of understanding. It stems from low self-esteem which, once raised, allows the judgement to stop. To judge another is a projection of self-judgement. It might give you a temporary illusion that you are better than another but in truth we are all of equal worth with differences to be appreciated, not judged.

I knew a couple whose relationship was dominated by judgement. The man constantly criticised the woman to the extent that she was terrified of his wrath. You might ask: why did she stick around? Unfortunately relationships can reach this state because although it is unhealthy, we get addicted to destructive habits. One of the hardest but most important abilities to develop is to face your relationship honestly; and in particular to admit to those areas that don't work.

Jane and Murray came to see me suffering from chronic judgement issues. Thankfully they had the courage to admit that their relationship wasn't working and they wanted to find a way out. When they explained the situation it was apparent that Jane judged Murray excessively, which caused him to react with anger. As a starting point I encouraged them to share their judgements with each other for the purpose of raising awareness and making new choices. It was important that we set clear boundaries for this exercise otherwise it could have just added to the dynamic already at work. They agreed to listen to each other without reacting, from which point they could then open a discussion to transform the judgement.

Jane spoke first. Her list of judgements included that Murray was too weak emotionally and not capable of standing up to others, that he didn't have a clear sense of direction in his life, that he was lazy and wasn't quick witted or clever enough. It was hard for Murray to hear these criticisms but even harder for him to divulge his. He felt that it was disloyal to reveal them but ultimately could see the sense of it. His judgements included that Jane was uncaring and bossy, that she was neurotic and didn't know how to enjoy life.

Once they had shared their lists we focused on the pay-offs that they got from holding on to their positions. A pay-off is an unconscious benefit that keeps the habit in place. Initially they couldn't see any because they claimed that they didn't want judgement wrecking their relationship, but upon deeper reflection they could see that there were some. Jane revealed how she was able to prove her belief that men are gullible, and that the way to stay in control was to put them down. She realised that she had made that decision from watching her father drink his life away. Subconsciously she had decided that she would never let her relationship fall in to that state and watched over Murray like a hawk. Murray realised that he had seen his parents' marriage governed by conflict. He vowed that he would take it easy and not end up in a constant battle. Their two stories dovetailed perfectly.

The next step was to agree on a strategy for resolving these stories. They committed to relinquish judgements and to focus on supporting each other. They agreed to look for the qualities they valued in each other, and share them together. They played a game called the 'right' day game, in which one person gets to be right for 24 hours. No matter what your partner says you agree with them, from what colour they say the sky is to what food for you are having for dinner. Playing this game allows you to see the absurdity of needing to be 'right' all the time and shows you that it's more important to be happy. They agreed to admit when they were still judging and learn to smile at it rather than make it real.

Notice in which areas you have a tendency to judge yourself and/or your partner and commit to giving it up. Relinquishing judgment brings you freedom and full self-expression. Think about how you respond when you are perceived in a constructive light. You shine, you play big and you relax. The choice to look for the best in your partner allows the relationship to flourish and move from strength to strength.

4

Set The Intention

THE PRINCIPLE OF CREATION

When I was sixteen I had the privilege of travelling to China with the Yehudi Menuhin School orchestra. We had two pupils from mainland China studying at the school, which was rare for a communist state. We had been invited to give concerts in Beijing and Shanghai and were eager to visit such a different culture and to see how other people lived. There were many scenes that left lasting impressions including the mass of bicycles and green uniforms moving down the streets, being surrounded by smiling faces as we walked around and the extraordinary range of food on offer.

There was one sight that truly touched me. Early in the morning in the parks and on street corners a variety of people from young children to the elderly were practising T'ai Chi. Such grace, flexibility and freedom seemed a stark contrast to the apparent rigidity of the rest of their existence. In retrospect I realised that what they were doing was setting an intention for each day. Practising T'ai Chi nourished and sustained them whilst living in a controlled environment.

We live in a land of relative freedom, but it doesn't always feel like that. The world can seem like a prison, and we can experience relationships as restricting and work as a heavy burden unless we place ourselves at the centre of creating our lives. This process starts by setting an intention to bring forth our vision and clarify our purpose. We then need to continue the commitment to let go of our past conditioning in order to make way for something new.

Decide how you want to be

We live in a crazy world. The common cry of many people today is 'stop the world – I want to get off!' But we can't. We are driven by the desire for 'more'; a condition at The Happiness Project we call *'more-osis'*. We have been led to believe that more money, more achievement, more sex, more status and more things will make us happy. We strive for more and yet more is never enough. This is backward thinking. We have turned into *human doings* and have forgotten that behind the busy schedule and hurried lifestyle we are *human beings*. By deciding how you want *to be* first, you create an opening for doing and having what you truly want.

I learnt this lesson on my quest for the ultimate relationship. I initially believed that if I did the 'right' things I would have the relationship of my dreams. I studied the books, listened to the tapes and went to the seminars. It certainly helped, but the big change came when I stopped trying to do the 'right' things and decided how I wanted to be. Mahatma Gandhi expressed this principle in his famous statement: *'Be the change that you want to see'*. Being is a choice. Being sets an example. Being is the expression of intention in action. All change begins with an intention and within it are the mechanics for its realisation. At this stage we do not need to know how it will happen. In fact, searching for this knowledge can prevent its manifestation. As we set an intention we align ourselves with the wisdom of creation, which is the same intelligence that created each one of us.

Before I met Veronica I hadn't figured out how I was going to meet the woman of my dreams. I had tried on many occasions, but to no avail; usually the more I tried, the more removed I became from it happening. Instead I began to be what I wanted to see in my life. I wanted love, so I became loving. I wanted friendship, so I became a good friend. I wanted fun, so I became fun to be with. I decided to be all that I could be. If you are trying hard to get a relationship or to improve one, stop! It doesn't work. Having a great relationship is first and foremost about *being* a great partner. Therefore, each day commit to being all that you can be.

When I did meet Veronica it was at a seminar entitled 'The Next Step'. It was a brief encounter which resumed a year later on a holiday in India after many expensive long-distance phone calls! Before seeing her again I distinctly remember setting the intention for how I wanted to be, and letting go of trying to work out what was going to happen. We talked, we laughed and we allowed the friendship to unfold. We trusted the unknown, we opened our hearts and we allowed our instincts to guide us. We both took the risk of being who we wanted to be with each other. I know that if I had become caught in the logistics of the relationship it wouldn't have worked. Veronica came from New Zealand and lived in Tokyo, while I lived in London. We were both highly independent and had enjoyed our single status. The odds were against us. Thankfully we stayed with our intention to be who we wanted to be, and the consequence was to live together and eventually marry.

Deciding how you want to be is a daily choice. It's not something that you do just once. I recommend upon awakening to check in with yourself and decide how you want to be that day. Decide what's important to you and commit to it. If love is important to you decide to be the presence of love. If joy is important to you decide to be joyful. If happiness is important to you decide to be happy. These qualities have innate intelligence. They embody a wisdom which extends itself to you. For example, ask love to guide you, to reveal itself to you and to show you how to be loving. Let the intelligence of love inspire your relationships, your communications and your actions.

Decision is power. Ask yourself: *'how do I want to be in my relationship?'* Deciding how *you* want to be eliminates the tendency to look outside yourself for fulfilment. It puts the emphasis back on yourself and acts as a map to guide you through your life and relationships.

Make your finishing line the starting line

How often do you catch yourself waiting for everything to work out in your relationship before you can be happy, loving and generous? We decide that we'll be happy when our partner is perfect, if they do everything we like, or when they meet our needs. The type of conditions that we place on a relationship set us up to be unhappy because as long as we base our happiness on external factors, we postpone it.

Making your finishing line the starting line means that you immediately set the intention for the ultimate goal of your relationship. You give up waiting, let go of conditions and decide just to be happy. On countless occasions I have worked with couples who put happiness at the end of the line; who agree unconsciously that they will not be happy unless all their conditions are met, some of which include:

Having a certain house.
Having to get the housework done.
Having x amount of money in the bank.
Driving a particular car.

These conditions construct barriers to happiness in a relationship. It is like taking a rain check on what you truly want and letting old habits continue. Consider the possibility of starting your relationship each day in the way that you would like it to be: relaxed, loving, intimate, fun, joyful and compassionate. You no longer need to wait to be happy together. Happiness waits for your welcome not for time. The relationship will not be perfect just because you have met your conditions. My favourite definition of a perfectionist is someone who only looks for the imperfection! If you look for a reason to postpone happiness, you'll find one; and if you look for a reason to enjoy your relationship now you'll find that too.

Bill and Joyce were a good example of this dynamic in action. In their first session they set out all the complaints they had about each other. Bill claimed that Joyce never understood him. She nagged him to tidy up, to dress a certain way, to see only particular friends and to eat certain food. Joyce said that Bill never listened to her, that he was only interested in himself and hardly ever spent any time with her.

I asked them how they would like their relationship to be. They shared their dreams of being happy together, laughing a lot, being best friends, mutually supportive and intimate. I then asked what they thought would need to happen in order to realise this. They presented another long list of ways in which the other would need to change – their conditions. We considered the options of working through each condition, or letting them go. They saw that their willingness to let go would bring them closer to how they wanted to be. I suggested that each day they joined in setting their intention to be happy together and let go of the old conditions. At first they complained that it couldn't be that easy. Having suffered in the past, how could they simply be happy now? I advised them to set the intention and be patient. Over the forthcoming weeks they began to experience a shift away from the past irritation to a new level of joy.

To make your finishing line your starting line is a choice to take responsibility for the health of your relationship. We often shy away from responsibility as we associate it with a sense of burden, pressure and expectation. No wonder it becomes unwelcome! However, there is another way to look at responsibility – the ability to respond. It gives us choice, which gives us freedom. I struggled with the idea of responsibility being a blessing. I thought that freedom meant being single because I was not accountable to anyone else. Eventually I realised that I hung on to my single status as a form of defence, to protect me from false fears. It kept me trapped in a vicious circle. Meeting Veronica gave me a new reference point for responsibility. I no longer saw it as a noose around my neck and I welcomed the challenge because of the growth and opportunity it brought me.

Making your finishing line the starting line is the ultimate act in taking responsibility for it. You no longer wait for circumstances to work out, for the household chores to get done or for the children to go to bed. You can decide to be close and intimate at any stage of being together. You can decide to let go and love at the beginning and end of each day. Making this choice nurtures and strengthens your partnership. It rekindles romance, breeds love and nurtures compassion. Without this focus a relationship can flounder, as there are many obstacles which can distract us from being in true partnership. Only you can make the choice to weather these obstacles with grace in order for your relationship to flourish.

Hit a reset button

With the best intention in the world it is easy to come off track. We decide to be loving and within minutes we lose it. We decide to be happy only to get frustrated over little things. This is part and parcel of the rich tapestry of life. As M. Scott Peck says in the opening line of *The Road Less Travelled*, 'Life is difficult.' He goes on to say that once we accept that life is difficult it no longer is. To accept the difficulties that a relationship brings makes it easier to navigate, and transforms your perception of it.

I have always found it immensely reassuring to discover that other people have a hard time in relationships. It is not that I want others to suffer – far from it! It's just that it makes my own journey more manageable when I realise that I'm not alone with my challenges. Often the main value of receiving professional help or reading a book about relationships is to see that you are not alone with your difficulties. We are all human beings with the quirks that make us unique.

The idea of hitting a reset button is to get back on track in your relationship when you lose your way. There are going to be times when you forget to decide how you want to be and you're caught waiting for happiness. This is okay. Every moment presents an opportunity to refocus, recommit and reconnect. The key point is your intention because it inspires the creation of what you seek. To hit a reset button is to recommit your intention.

In my marriage I have found myself sometimes having to hit a reset button many times in one day! There was one period when we were both stressed. We had been working long hours, redecorating the house and we had not taken a holiday for some time. We were irritable with each other and short-tempered. We had slipped into a routine of waiting for things to get better. The excuses came thick and fast; 'if only we had more time', 'we can relax once the pressure's off'. Eventually we reminded each other about the tyranny of the WAIT problem, (waiting to be happy), and chose to hit a reset button for peace each time we lost it. Initially it didn't appear to make a big difference, but the continued commitment paid off. We began to experience peace again without any circumstances having changed. It was cheaper than a holiday, readily available and a joy to do.

Hitting a reset button strengthens your commitment to the core values which guide your relationship. I worked with a couple called Angela and Charles who applied this principle at a difficult time. They wanted to have a child but were unable to conceive. It put a great strain on the relationship as they questioned their compatibility and future together. At first they were mutually supportive but as time went on they found it too painful to discuss. They closed down emotionally and immersed themselves in their work.

One of the first things I asked them to do was to share their values, the backbone of the relationship. They disclosed very similar values including love, honesty, companionship, freedom and fun. As a result of their difficulties they had put these on a back burner. Their main goal was to get through the day. This is a common scenario at stressful times, but unless we remember what matters to us it is hard to transcend it. Angela and Charles agreed to hit a reset button to remind them of specific values. They took a different one each week and decided to remind each other of it whenever they slipped back into a survival mode. For example, one week they agreed to focus on love. Putting love at the forefront of their relationship helped them to be kind and compassionate with each other and gave their problems a new perspective. Another week they agreed to practise acceptance. This allowed them to continue their relationship with respect and understanding.

We are creative beings. Hitting a reset button is one of the keys to using our creativity. It aligns us with natural laws of creation. Nature continues to grow and flourish even in the harshest of conditions. I am often amazed to see the power of a plant as it reaches for life in a concrete city. It doesn't struggle with life. It flows with life. We can learn to connect with this natural flow, which strengthens our trust and provides us with further resources at difficult times.

Commit to hitting a reset button if you have found that you've come off track. Ask yourself: *'What am I really committed to here? What is my intention here?'* Remember: accepting that relationships will have their difficulties gives you a powerful reference point for keeping things in perspective.

Get creative

If you ever questioned your creative powers, think again! A relationship is a creative act and being in a relationship is one of the most creative things you could ever do. In every moment you create love or fear, passion or pain, intimacy or separation, joy or conflict. Life is all about duality and it is up to you what you create. The foundation of creativity lies in your perception. Before you read on take a look at the following statement:

OPPORTUNITYISNOWHERE

Did you read: 'opportunity is nowhere', or 'opportunity is now here?' The law of perception says be careful what you look for because you'll find it! If you look for opportunity you will find it and if you look for an absence of it you'll find that too. In a relationship your creativity influences how you perceive that relationship. Do you perceive a relationship as a source of inspiration, or a block? Do you look for love, or wait for it? Do you see the gifts that your partner has to offer, or the difficulties?

One of the great traps we fall into is tunnel vision, seeing only as far as our beliefs. I was once eating in a restaurant listening to a couple's conversation (to evesdrop has always held a fascination for me!). The lady was talking about a potential work opportunity. Her communication was animated and she was obviously looking to her partner for encouragement and support. In response she received a long list of potential pitfalls and discouragement. She visibly drooped as he continued to search for evidence why she shouldn't proceed with the opportunity. She tried to stand up for her beliefs but he knocked her down each time. Instead of supporting her in seeing the opportunity, unfortunately he gave an opinion which lacked imagination and squashed her enthusiasm.

The essence of my work is to help people see things differently. To experience a breakthrough in your perception involves willingness and creativity. This combination opens us to new possibilities. Each day presents small ways to be creative. For example, in your relationship do you sleep on the same side of the bed night after night? If so, be willing to swap sides to break the routine. One client of mine was reluctant to hear this news. She was very attached to her side of the bed and did not want to swap. Her partner welcomed it as he found that he had interesting dreams the few times that he had slept on her side! Do you have a morning routine that has become predictable? If so, decide how you can spice it up. Maybe wake up ten minutes earlier so you can have some quiet time together. Put aside the morning paper and mail to have an enjoyable breakfast conversation. Do you ever have a spontaneous lunch date during the working week? If not, spot an opportunity and grab it. Has your evening schedule become dominated by television or working late? If so, unplug the TV, get home on time, cook an exotic meal and celebrate.

One day I received the following e-mail that I found amusing: 'Normal life is getting dressed in clothes that you buy for work, driving through traffic in a car that you are still paying for in order to get to the job that you need so you can pay for the clothes, car and the house that you leave empty all day in order to afford to live in it!'

If you relate to this scenario it's definitely time to get creative. Start by setting the intention. Commit daily to a life and relationship fuelled by creativity. We arrive into the world from an act of creation and we can continue it. Don't get tied up in figuring out how you're going to be creative; it doesn't mean that you have to be an artist. Creativity is simply a part of you which, brought in to your relationship, transforms it.

From now on, train your mind to spot the opportunity in situations. Be willing to look at things differently. Be open to new ideas and new possibilities. Whenever you are feeling blocked ask yourself: *'If I were to be creative right now, what would I do, where would I go, what would I say, and to whom?'* As Helen Keller said, 'Life is either a daring adventure or it is nothing at all.' Having the courage to follow your creativity opens yourself up to inspiration, innovation and passion.

Let your intention guide you

I once heard the story of a ship's captain seeing a light at sea. He sent out a message for the carrier of the light to move. The message came back asking the ship to alter its own course. The captain was furious and replied that his was a great ship and that they must move immediately. The message was returned: 'You are a great ship and I am the lighthouse!' Intention functions as a lighthouse. It sends out a ray of light that you can follow if you choose. It has an innate intelligence, which will guide you and your relationship if you let it. Intention is also creative. It is a source of inspiration from which great deeds flow.

A couple I know are an inspiration in relation to letting intention guide them. Tom and Claire have a fulfilling and loving partnership. They are a source of strength to many people to whom they open their home and hearts. When I asked how they are able to give so much to others and have room left for themselves, without hesitation they replied that their intention carries them forward. They set the intention to give love and to receive it. They then surrender to it rather than impose their own will. Their motto in life is: 'Thy will, not my will.'

In order to have a loving and intimate relationship, allow your intention to guide you. Schedule some quiet time for listening to the guidance intention offers you. Learn to become mindful for a day, noticing when you remember to follow this guidance and when you forget. I recognise guidance as a voice in my head that has a serene quality to it. Other people see pictures or images, whilst others will feel it. This guidance is your intuition, or 'inner-tuition'. It is available to you 24 hours a day. People also talk about it as a gut feeling or an inner knowing, and letting it guide you ensures that you are on purpose in life.

A common stereotype is that women are more intuitive than men. I believe that it's more socially acceptable for women to be intuitive, but men are intuitive too. In one anonymous survey taken in America of male executives of the top performing companies, over 70% said that they made their major decisions on intuition as well as fact. To follow your intuition requires you to let go and trust and adds a new dimension to a relationship. The experience of synchronicity, or coincidence, becomes commonplace as you become more in tune with each other. You tap into the creative potential of the relationship and breathe new life into it.

Letting your intention guide you also gives you a further strategy for handling conflict when it emerges. Instead of seeing the conflict as a problem, you are able to listen closely to what it is telling you. Maybe it is an invitation to change. It might be telling you that there is some disharmony in your life that you need to address. Maybe you need to slow down, take your foot off the accelerator and look at your priorities.

Relationships require time to thrive. In order to feel and express love, to share experiences and thoughts, to understand each other, you need to spend time together looking at the sunset, dawdling on the walk to school, watching old movies on a Sunday afternoon, chatting, throwing pebbles into a stream. Commit to letting your intention guide you. Listen to your intuition. What is it telling you? Take the guidance that it offers and trust it. Your ego will fall away, giving you new clarity, fresh vision and greater opportunity.

The choice to let go

One of the greatest obstacles to having a creative relationship is our inability to let go. To let go means that you are flexible, able to see all sides of a situation, willing to drop your personal agenda and to stop resisting what is good for you. Our capacity to hold on, resist and be stubborn never ceases to amaze me. The major block to letting go is fear, and the greatest benefit is peace.

Since the ego would rather be right about the belief in lack, conflict and separation, we need to stay constantly vigilant in order to prevent it from dominating our relationships. Whenever you catch yourself searching for something, check to see whether you are being controlled by your ego. You will know because you experience no peace, no happiness and no fulfilment. Allow this to be a reminder to let go and return to your higher self.

The higher self is the part of you that has been untouched by past conditioning. Picture the sun. It is always shining and radiant. We don't always see it because of clouds, rain, snow and storms, however this does not mean that it has disappeared. It has temporarily been covered. In this analogy the sun is your higher self and the clouds are the ego. Whenever you are caught in a storm use it as a reminder to return to your higher self. This gives a sense of purpose to the craziness that we can experience. It is simply a powerful lesson to let go. Learning these lessons strengthens our experience of the higher self and by continuing to do so, we create our own internal sunshine, whatever the conditions outside.

It is essential within a relationship to develop this capacity to let go. There will be challenges and obstacles to overcome but your willingness to let go is the key to successfully navigating these events. Letting go is a choice for the best thing to prevail. It demonstrates that you believe in yourself enough not to have to prove your opinions at the expense of the relationship.

Ron and Mary came to see me at a difficult time in their relationship. Ron had been offered a promotion which required him to travel and work longer hours. He wanted to take it to advance his career, but when he tried to discuss it with Mary she became angry and aloof. When we examined the deeper issues it was revealed that Mary was upset because of the way he had communicated the promotion. From her perspective Ron had told her the news as a *fait accompli*. She felt that she had not been consulted and she was concerned about the ramifications of the change. I asked him to communicate his side of the story. He said that he had simply shared his excitement of the news but found her reaction so negative that he became defensive. He revealed that he was afraid that Mary would oppose the move and felt that he had to assert his will without taking her feelings into account.

By discussing their opinions they realised that they were both afraid and acting defensively. Their egos had taken over and prevented them from seeing the issue objectively. We talked about the role that letting go could play. They agreed to practise listening to their higher self. When we connect with the higher self we're able to bring trust into a situation, which deepens our ability to let go. This enabled Ron and Mary to understand each other more fully. He could appreciate her fears and she recognised how important the offer was to him. The final upshot was that he agreed to negotiate the promotion in order to have relative control over the amount of time he travelled and for them to schedule time together so they had a healthy balance.

This type of softening process allows room for change to occur. When we hold on too tightly it restricts growth and expansion. Ask yourself: *'How can I let go in my relationship?'* Applying this can initially take you out of your comfort zone. Your continuous commitment to it ensures that it becomes easier and brings you the rewards of love and trust.

Create true partnership

One of the greatest gifts that a relationship offers is true partnership. It fulfils our desire for companionship, support, love and intimacy. It also strengthens our self-image because to have someone believing in you helps you to believe in yourself. When I reflect on how far Veronica and I have come since our partnership began it astounds me. I believe that her love and support have accelerated the happiness and success of my life and that I have contributed to hers in a similar vein. (I did take the risk of checking it out and she gave positive confirmation!)

The greatest obstacle to creating true partnership is the dynamic of independence. We have been led to believe that to be independent is an ultimate sign of freedom. The independent person strives to do everything on their own, to be a one man/ woman show. Not only do they want to write, direct, produce and star in the movie of their life, they want to run around and organise all the props as well. They reject support, and push love away. To try and stay independent and have an intimate relationship just doesn't work. It appears too threatening so the independent person will get out of the relationship and tell themselves that they had a lucky escape. However, to develop a functional relationship we need to recognise that independence is a stage along the route to creating true partnership and that we have to go beyond it to join with someone at a deeper level.

The primary characteristic of true partnership is a state of interdependency. To choose to become interdependent is to be capable of building a rich, enduring and meaningful relationship. It is to accept the painful and frustrating times and to understand that they can contribute to the health of the relationship if we choose to let them. Interdependency recognises that your relationship is a gift and that it brings greater rewards than you experienced on your own.

It takes strong intention and a large amount of willingness to create interdependency. It is often at the point when a relationship could take a significant leap in partnership that we decide to quit. As the saying goes, 'when the going gets tough, the tough get going!' To be clear on your intention and commit to interdependency when things get tough pulls you through.

To develop interdependency requires a major commitment. It doesn't happen by itself. Through effective communication, understanding your partner and choosing to let go, you move towards it. There is a steep learning curve involved, which is why you often hear in a successful relationship that the early days were the most difficult. Although you have the excitement of the 'honeymoon' period, in which your partner can do no wrong, getting used to another person's eccentricities and giving up independence can take some time.

Dave was a confirmed bachelor. He had a high-flying job in the financial markets and enjoyed a fast lifestyle. He was always the life and soul of a party, charming everyone he met. As a result he had a large circle of friends, some of whom tried to fix him up with a partner at every opportunity. I was surprised that he came to see me because he appeared to lead such a good life and genuinely to enjoy it. It soon became apparent that underneath the bold exterior was a man wanting true partnership. He revealed how he had been devastated by the break-up of his first major relationship in his early twenties. He decided that it was better to stay independent but now realised that it was a cover up for his fear of intimacy. Whenever a relationship became too close for comfort he would end it. Naturally he wanted a fast track to change this pattern.

I encouraged him to start being honest and authentic in his relationships. This was a big challenge because he usually ended a relationship before there was time to disclose his true feelings. He feared that he would hurt women's feelings and that it would cause conflict. He agreed to do it anyway and despite the initial discomfort he was surprised by the results. Women welcomed his greater honesty. They began to open up themselves and he had conversations he'd only imagined were possible. He discovered that many women also thrived on their independence but yearned for greater meaning and partnership.

He found that as long as he stayed honest and clear about his intentions he could maintain different friendships. The crunch came when he met someone with whom he fell deeply in love. He was shocked to find that he really wanted the relationship to work. It became the highest priority in his life. Everything else took a back seat as he opened to a new type of experience. He began to be a man of his word, keeping the commitments and promises that he made, whereas in the past he had thought nothing of breaking them. He attended to little things that touch the heart and show that you truly care, something he had never paid attention to previously. He apologised when he made mistakes and he took responsibility in areas where previously he would have passed the buck. These are all actions that build true partnership. They develop a level of trust, loyalty and integrity, which sustain a relationship.

Be willing to go beyond independence. Notice any old wounds and grievances you hold that prevent you from creating true partnership, and be willing to let them go. Reflect on how it would feel if you let your partner fully support you. Imagine healing past defences and being open and free today. You are creative and you can create the relationship of your dreams. By focusing on true partnership you turn that possibility into a reality.

5

Fear Less, Talk More

THE PRINCIPLE OF COMMUNICATION

Before I met Veronica I had developed a habit in relationships of never saying what I really wanted to say. I didn't want to give too much information away, I was afraid of what other people would think, revealing my feelings, causing possible confrontation, and not being understood. I created elaborate ways of talking around issues, avoiding the point, being elusive and sounding convincing. I survived but it was unsatisfying. I was pretending to communicate but there was no authenticity, my heart and soul were missing. The consequence was that my relationships were shallow affairs, never reaching beyond a certain point of intimacy.

I remember at the beginning of my relationship with Veronica making the decision to be bold – to speak my mind, to communicate from my heart and to let her know my intimate thoughts and feelings. It felt risky, and on many occasions it would have been easier to keep my mouth shut, but I knew that to communicate was more important. Veronica was also ready for this level of communication and over the years it has continued to develop, creating greater empathy and understanding. This has provided a strong level of trust so that when there are difficult issues to discuss, and problems arise we have a firm foundation to fall back upon.

How do you communicate? The following questions are designed for you to reflect upon your communication style:

◆ Do you ignore people by interrupting their sentences, talking when you've lost interest in what they are saying and/or not waiting for answers in response to a question?

◆ Do you pretend to communicate by saying what you think you 'should' say, saying what you think the receiver wants to hear and/or paying more attention to the conversation in your own mind than to what is being said?

◆ Do you select your communication by hearing things that interest you, blocking out what doesn't and saying only what you want to say?

◆ Are you an attentive communicator who nods your head in the right places, looks keen and interested and/or speaks with enthusiasm?

◆ Are you an empathic communicator who is honest, authentic and speaks from your heart, who genuinely listens to what is being said without filtering it through your past perceptions and who has the capacity to project into the other person's world?

These examples relate to the five main levels of communication. They are:

1. **Ignoring**. This is when you refuse to take notice of another. It is the result of not being interested in what is being said or an attempt to control someone. There are occasions when we have to ignore in order to filter out an overload of information, or to get on with our lives, but to ignore your partner is a recipe for disaster.

2. **Pretending**. To feign communication is an unsatisfactory experience. Although we often use pretence in social or business contexts when we think we should be interested in something and we're not, it provides no depth and is exhausting. To pretend in an intimate relationship creates a false impression that can be difficult to break once it becomes a habit.

3. **Selecting**. You listen to what you want to hear and filter out the rest. You say what you want to say and leave the rest unsaid. To communicate in a selective manner leaves room for misunderstanding and detrimental consequences further

down the line. It keeps you closed in your own world and prevents you from seeing things as they really are.

4. **Attending**. Attentive communication looks good. You appear to be interested, speak sincerely but it lacks a true quality of engagement or authenticity. It's as though you are doing all the right things to communicate but without any heart or soul.

5. **Being empathic**. To communicate with empathy means that you have the ability to project yourself into and fully understand another. It provides the foundation for a secure, honest and dynamic relationship because the level of trust ensures that both people can relate to each other fully.

I asked countless people what they regarded as the most important ingredient for a successful relationship. The overwhelming response was communication. However, it amazes me how often we think we're communicating effectively when we're not. We filter what people say, we edit our own conversation and find the idea of expressing ourselves threatening. This has a high cost for a relationship. Without good communication trust breaks down, love diminishes, joy evaporates, intimacy disappears. Communication failure is at the heart of most relationship breakdowns. Therefore learning the art of communication is the essence of an intelligent relationship.

Express yourself

Imagine being able to express yourself fully and freely. Consider the benefits of finding your voice, saying what you think and feel, without worrying about what other people think. So often it is our fear of others' opinions that prevents us from expressing ourselves fully. These fears include: worrying that people won't like us, that we will cause upset, that we will hurt another's feelings, that we will be over-bearing, and that we will appear unintelligent. They are decisions which we made as a result of past experiences, which can still affect us today.

Cast your mind back to your childhood. What messages did

you receive from your parents and/or adult influences about expressing yourself? Common phrases such as: 'children should be seen and not heard', 'keep quiet and you won't get into trouble', 'there will be tears before bedtime', or being told to 'shutup' created the fear of self-expression. This is a great contrast to today's society where children are usually encouraged to speak up, give their opinion and be taken seriously.

A further unhelpful influence might have been the lack of good role models in communication. Perhaps your parents tended either to favour not expressing themselves, or communicated in a verbally abusive way. Maybe your teachers had a dictatorial approach that was fear-based and discouraged speaking up. In the workplace hierarchal systems created a culture that also dampened self-expression. Reversing the impact of these influences brings you a new experience of communication.

Some people have the knack of expressing themselves with no difficulty. They are comfortable talking about themselves, giving their opinions, laughing and crying. They get things off their chest and they handle conflict comfortably. Think for a moment who is the most effective communicator you know personally and why. What characteristics and qualities enable them to express themselves confidently?

I have a friend called Tony who is an extraordinary communicator. He has the ability to connect with everyone and enjoys a deeply rewarding relationship with his partner. This wasn't always the case. When I first met him he found it extremely challenging to express his thoughts and feelings. His parents had been autocratic in their approach to child-rearing and he had learned to hold his tongue. As an adult he struggled to create relationships because he felt so threatened at the prospect of having to communicate.

Tony made it a priority to transform his communication. He was an introvert by nature therefore conversation did not come easily. He was introduced to a communication model, which he used as a blueprint to develop his skills. Called the B.E. P.O.S.I.T.I.V.E model it is a useful reminder about which qualities are involved:

- Breath – breathe well
- Eyes – engage with your eyes
- Posture – relax your posture
- Openness – be open, without defence
- Smile – be warm, use humour
- Interest – listen with interest
- Time – take time to communicate
- Image – self-image and appearance are important
- Voice – quality and intonation
- Empathy – learning to connect, understand before you are understood

By applying these ideas Tony took giant steps towards his current position, working as a public speaker. Given that public speaking is one of the greatest fears we have, Tony has been an inspiration to me about what is possible. He has learnt to breathe deeply and in a relaxed way; he is comfortable at maintaining eye contact, without turning it into a staring contest; he has an upright and relaxed posture; he is honest and accepting, enabling him to be open; he loves to laugh and be playful; he takes a genuine interest in others; he makes communication a priority therefore if he doesn't have time he makes it; he has a healthy self-image and enjoys dressing well; he has a voice that you could listen to all day and seeks to understand others, building a good rapport.

Even if you have a quiet personality it is vitally important for the health of your relationship to speak up. Your partner is not a mind-reader. Although they might be tuned in to your needs, choosing to express yourself can save much heartache and misunderstanding. I worked with a client who put this into practice. Married with a seven-month-old child, Lucy suffered periods of exhaustion from lack of sleep. Whenever these occasions arose she became 'needy' which her husband found difficult to handle. She would feel insecure, nervy, and shaky inside. She expected her husband to understand her feelings without explaining how she felt and resented it when he didn't. She felt guilty about wanting to rest during the day, telling herself that she should press on with her 'to do' list. Having this awareness enabled Lucy to tell her husband what was going on and then to pre-empt any future upset by expressing how she felt before it had built up. She was concerned that he would see this as further pressure, but in fact the opposite was true. He welcomed the explanation and was relieved about not having to exercise psychic powers.

To express yourself requires you to take responsibility for your thoughts and feelings. It is essential not to blame your partner for your experience. Responding with blame results in conflict and hurt. For example, there is a world of difference between saying: 'In the situation involving x you hurt my feelings' and 'In the situation involving x I felt hurt'. The first version is blaming your partner for how you feel whereas in the second you take ownership of your feelings and do not use your partner as a dumping ground.

Another important aspect of expressing yourself is being sensitive to others' needs. We have probably all known people who carry on talking when others around them have lost interest. To carry that into your intimate relationship is not a wise choice. Your partner can feel overwhelmed by your outpouring and frustrated by your inability to heed warning signs that now is not a good time. Getting the balance right between expressing yourself and listening requires you to trust that there is enough space and time to be heard. We all have a deep need to be listened to, and if it has not been met in the past, it can lead to compulsive talking.

A useful way to learn how you come across is to ask your partner for feedback. Discovering how they perceive the way you express yourself can be revealing. It is easier for others to be objective about us; we are too emotionally involved and fail to recognise the ways that we can improve in this area. When you receive feedback listen to it before responding. Let it sink in so that you can reflect upon it without giving an immediate response. Asking for feedback also gives your partner the opportunity to express themselves in constructive ways and deepens trust within the relationship.

The true art of self-expression is to be authentic. Being authentic is to communicate from your heart, so that people are genuinely moved by what you say. It requires you to be honest, defenceless and courageous. It also means that you have to admit when you are being inauthentic, or not being real. You can identify this if you have slipped into playing a role, trying to look good or pretending. You are able to tell if someone is being inauthentic by not being able to believe what they're saying. It might appear that they are saying the 'right' thing, or what you want to hear, but it doesn't feel genuine to you.

One man I worked with feared that his partner was having an affair. He asked her on several occasions if there was any truth to his suspicions. Each time she reassured him that it was a complete illusion, that she would never have an affair. He didn't believe her but continued the relationship anyway. Eventually he discovered that she was having an affair. The aspect that was most painful was her deceit in the situation. He said that if she had had the courage to admit it, although he would have been upset, he would not have been left with such a sense of betrayal.

People often disguise their fear of being authentic by trying to justify that it's better not to say anything and rock the boat. I have seen relationships and families torn apart for years by this type of behaviour. The irony is that people generally know what's going on anyway, even if it hasn't been said.

Ask yourself: *how could I be more authentic and more honest in the way I communicate?* The commitment to expressing yourself and being authentic in a relationship opens up new possibilities of love, intimacy, vitality, and joy. It creates the freedom to be yourself and gives your partner the gift of who you really are.

Listen up!

Pause for a moment and listen to the voice in your head. You're probably asking yourself, 'what voice in my head, what's he going on about now? I don't have a voice in my head. He must be crazy.' Yes, that's the one, the voice that gives a running commentary whether you're reading a book, watching a movie or listening to someone talking. It's like having the commentary to the horseracing going on 24 hours a day. In fact it's rare to listen to what someone is saying because you're either telling yourself what they're saying or waiting to talk yourself. Just because you have been blessed with an ability to 'hear' is not the same thing as being able to 'listen'.

There are two main types of listening: *passive listening*, or nodding, waiting to reply, hearing without understanding, and *active listening*, or empathising with your partner. Empathy is created by your willingness to put yourself in their shoes and understand their reality. As we all have our own unique perception about life, your ability to see things the way they do develops a deep understanding and a sense for them of having been met.

There are four main steps to active listening. They are: listen to what your partner says without interrupting; reflect back to them what you think you've heard; ask them if you have understood fully and listen to any other response that they may have.

I witnessed an example of active listening with some close friends. They were discussing where to go on holiday and trying to meet each other's needs. Emily said she was dreaming of a sun-drenched holiday by the beach to rejuvenate. She shared how she was feeling drained by her busy lifestyle and wanted to get away from it all. She expressed her concern that Don, her partner, would get bored and not want to go. Don paid close attention whilst listening to her and then reflected back to her what he had heard. He said that she wanted to take a quiet, restful holiday in a sunny climate but was worried that he wouldn't enjoy it and not want to go. He didn't jump in to defend his position or interpret in any way. He asked her if he had understood, to which she replied that he had. Emily then shared that, having expressed her concerns, she was not so attached to the type of holiday they took, but that it was far more important that they had an enjoyable time together. It often happens that once you have expressed your position and been fully listened to, you become more flexible and recognise the heart of the issue.

Having listened to Emily, Don then expressed his opinion. He said that although he enjoyed visiting warm countries he found seaside resorts limiting. He preferred a location where he could walk and explore the countryside as well. Emily listened to his position and reflected it back correctly, which allowed him to agree that the priority was their happiness together rather than where they went. This demonstrates that when real listening takes place and people feel understood it opens up win/win possibilities that were previously hidden.

The major obstacle to active listening is that it takes conscious effort. Passive listening can appear far easier because you can pretend to listen whilst staying in your own world. This can work as a quick fix but creates a rocky context as soon as anything important arises. If someone does not feel heard, arguments start which can spiral out of control. Some of the deepest human needs are to be understood, to be validated and to be appreciated, and if these are not met within a relationship the bonding breaks and cracks materialise. Active listening provides the glue that binds a relationship together. It provides the foundation from which it can build and soar to new heights.

Developing your active listening skills takes practice and patience. I never cease to be amazed at how rewarding it is, once achieved. Marriage has certainly given me the opportunity to reap the benefits. When I first met Veronica I was dying to know her life story. I listened for hours as she revealed her experiences and reflections. We became great friends as we opened our hearts. It all went smoothly until we had to make life-changing decisions together. As our personal realities became challenged the temptation to impose our own individual wills grew stronger. Tension occurred as we attempted to work it out. I learnt that ceasing to interpret each other's position and committing to listening and projecting into each other's worlds resolved the major differences.

As a coach one of my main challenges is to create a listening environment. This is a space in which someone is listened to with acceptance and the commitment to be understood. I have noticed that it is easier to listen to others when I am not emotionally attached, but that it is harder when I am directly involved, for example in my marriage or with family. The process of detaching from what is being said enables you to be more present to your partner when you are faced with difficulties. In order to develop detachment, witness your own thoughts and feelings. Observe them as if you were a neutral party, which enables you to step back and be objective.

Remember that if you do forget to listen actively, apologise quickly. We all make mistakes but we can learn from them. To apologise is to say that you are genuinely sorry for making assumptions, pretending to hear or feeding back your own opinion. It is an act of love to say sorry. It is an expression of love to listen.

Go beyond words

Studies in communication estimate that approximately 7% of our communication is through the words we speak. They reveal that a further 35% is represented by the pace and tone of our voice and the remaining 58% by our body language. Therefore to develop an intelligent relationship requires you to go beyond the words you speak and hear and to communicate with your whole being. The old saying, 'it's not what you say, it's how you say it' accords well with this theory.

One of the simplest and most powerful ways to experience communication beyond words is to spend time in silence with your partner. I remember an occasion with Veronica while we were visiting Nepal. We were sitting in a lovely restaurant over-looking Lake Pokhara, a beautiful location with the Annapurna range of mountains in the distance. We had spent the past couple of weeks travelling in India and it was our first opportunity to unwind. For some reason the atmosphere between us was tense. We were getting on each other's nerves; everything we said sparked a reaction. We agreed to stop talking and to be silent. As we sat there our body language softened, we uncrossed our arms and legs and we were able to resume eye contact. A sense of stillness occurred between us which was made possible by ceasing to talk. Our defences dropped and our hearts opened. We saw each other again as friends and were able to enjoy the silence, as well as the peace and warm feelings that came from it.

You do not need to be in a beautiful location to allow silence to weave its magic. By introducing silence into your relationship on a daily basis you gain the benefit of going beyond words. This enables you to become more sensitive to your partner's energy and helps you to stand back and observe the relationship. The ability to witness your relationship means that you can be more objective and resolving issues becomes easier. It is difficult to resolve conflict when feelings are running high. We can say things that we later regret. Taking silence creates a window of opportunity to reflect, calm down and to recommence communication with greater understanding.

The practice of going beyond words encourages you to look for the meaning behind your partner's words. To develop this ability requires a willingness and sensitivity to listen on all levels. It is similar to communicating with a child before they can talk. Learning to read their body language, facial expressions and the intonation of their voice gives you clues to meeting their needs.

Growing up as a musician gave me direct experience of communicating beyond words; in particular the art of playing chamber music, which requires you to listen and respond with a particular deftness. In order for it to work you have to let go of a stubborn position and embrace a flexible outlook. Imagine your relationship to be a work of art. When you look at a picture you communicate beyond words. By projecting yourself into the artist's reference point, you notice colours, textures and images which enable you to connect with the message it conveys.

Begin to look at your partner in a new light. Ask yourself what they are communicating beyond the words they use. People start to talk about the experience of synchronicity as they put this into practice. I have some close friends who are masters of communicating beyond words. Each day they take some time to be silent together, usually either first thing in the morning or last thing at night. They find that it helps to keep the relationship clear of any emotional debris. They have also noted that they often share the same thoughts at this time when they recount what was on their mind. It strengthens their relationship because they develop ways of communicating that do not rely on words. When they spend time apart they keep a strong connection and often find that they telephone each other at exactly the same time or later relate that they were sharing similar feelings at a particular moment.

As you go beyond words you begin to develop greater sensitivity to your partner's communication style. Each of us has preferences for the way we send and receive information. Some people are more kinaesthetic, or feel things acutely on an emotional level. Others tend to be more visual, or their communication is dominated by what they see. Others are more auditory, and inclined to respond to the timbre, speed and volume of what is being said.

To discover you and your partner's preference begin to notice the words that you use. A kinaesthetic communicator will talk in terms of feelings: 'I feel that you are trying to tell me something', 'I sense that you are not comfortable', or 'I am not sure I'm following you'. Someone who is a visual communicator talks in terms of seeing: 'I see your point', 'My picture of you is blurred', or 'It seems pretty unclear to me'. An auditory person talks in terms of hearing: 'I hear what you are saying', 'It sounds as though you are unhappy', or 'That doesn't ring a bell'. Developing this awareness allows you to become closer together. Having the flexibility to communicate according to the preference of your partner creates greater understanding and rapport.

Take the time

One of the greatest obstacles to developing good communication is lack of time. There is no doubt that when we do not take the time to communicate fully in a relationship we pay the price.

Understanding breaks down, resentment builds and ultimately the level of trust is affected. Since time is a very precious commodity today it becomes of even greater significance to prioritise communication in your relationship. Unless you commit to scheduling time together it will not happen of its own accord. There will always seem to be more pressing deadlines than making time to communicate.

Recently some close friends decided to create time together for communication. They have three children and run their own business, therefore spending quality time together was not easy to do. They decided to follow the principle of 'Sharpen the Saw' from Stephen Covey's book *The 7 Habits of Highly Effective People*. Sharpening the saw is the habit of renewal without which a relationship suffers. Picture yourself going for a walk in a large forest and coming across a man who is working very hard cutting down trees. You stop to greet him and ask what he is doing. He replies in an impatient voice, 'Can't you see, I'm busy cutting down trees'. You look around the vast area where he is sawing and exclaim that it is a lot of work. He says that he has already put in long hours but has many more to go. You happen to notice that the blade on his saw is blunt and suggest that he take a break to sharpen it. He looks taken aback at this proposal, and says, 'I don't have time to sharpen the saw, I'm too busy sawing.'

Mary and Carl decided to take an afternoon off each week to sharpen the saw of communication. Initially they feared that their business would suffer and that important tasks would cause them to cancel this allocated time. They made the commitment anyway and agreed to vary the ways in which they spent their time. Sometimes they stayed at home sitting on the sofa talking and listening; at other times they went for long walks and let nature support their communication and on other occasions they participated in each other's favourite activities, such as shopping or visiting an art gallery.

On one occasion they had a conflict that highlighted their communication troubles. Mary had been talking about a personal preoccupation whilst Carl had tried to feign interest but was caught up in thinking about work. Finally, Mary became quite upset. She claimed that he never showed real interest in her and that even when they had made the time to be together his attention was elsewhere. Carl became defensive and tried to justify his position. This was the area where their saws had become blunt. They had neglected to understand each other enough and had drained their emotional reservoir. They had tried to cut corners to please each other and keep things on an even keel. Now they were paying the price. In order to restore honesty and trust for real communication to take place they had to take the time to face the issues in a constructive way.

Simply scheduling ten minutes a day for effective communication will sharpen your saw. I find the best time to do this is last thing at night. A good format is to decide which one of you is going to talk first whilst the other listens. The person talking first simply expresses what they would like to communicate whilst their partner actively listens without comment. When they have finished you switch over, leaving room for any debate or discussion once you have both expressed yourselves. It is important not to take unresolved matters to bed with you. By clearing anything at the end of each day you prevent issues from getting out of perspective. If disagreement or conflict does arise the following suggestions are designed to help:

◆ Focus on one issue at a time. It's important to be aware of the domino effect, when one issue turns into every issue that you've been unhappy with.

◆ If you do not accept responsibility for how you feel, you will not be able to respond in a constructive way. You will be reactive and blaming.

◆ Always use 'I' and not 'You' statements. This ensures that you own what you say.

◆ Make sure the timing is right. This is a challenge if you are in the heat of the moment, but agreeing to resolve a conflict later can give you necessary breathing space.

◆ Beware of blaming. All blame is out of order. It is a form of attack that you will have to defend and does not provide solutions.

◆ Check to see if you are making requests or demands. You are perfectly entitled to make requests, which may be refused however; making demands is a recipe for trouble.

◆ Are you being assertive or aggressive? Being assertive is taking a stand for what you believe; aggression is using force to get agreement.

◆ Be careful not to over-generalise. Using statements such as: 'You always', or 'You never', takes issues out of context.

◆ Don't assume. It's only too easy to make assumptions that lead to making an **ass** out of **u** and **me**.

◆ Give air-time. Listening not fixing is the way forward.

Ultimately taking the time to communicate is an investment in the future of your relationship. It builds trust, strengthens friendship and creates a deeply nurturing and fulfilling partnership.

Be patient

Patience is a virtue and in communication it is a lifeline. To develop the quality of patience means that you are willing to extend unconditional love, forgiveness and flexibility, which contribute to an intelligent relationship. The challenge is that as we live in a culture which promotes being busy, hurried and stressed, it is easy to slip into the trap of treating life as an emergency.

An intelligent relationship treats communication as a gift. It values each exchange and instead of rushing through life like a train, it is prepared to invest time, energy and effort in seeking understanding and compassion. To develop patience means that we approach the challenges in our relationships with an open heart and mind. We suspend our own opinion and project into our partner's world. Nobody responds well to hearing a point of view expressed in an impatient manner. We become reactive and might turn away from our partner, creating the very opposite of what we want to achieve. Being patient allows a relationship to develop at its own pace and brings respect and calm into situations.

I worked with a couple who were struggling with being patient. New to their relationship, they had high expectations and argued over the smallest issue. Neither of them exercised patience in their communication, which became fraught with tension. I encouraged them to be aware when they were communicating without patience and to notice the main triggers. They discovered that the primary drive was fear and that the way they controlled it was to be impatient. They agreed to practise being patient by taking some deep breaths before responding to each other. Although it felt artificial, creating this space allowed them to think before they spoke. It prevented them from saying things that they didn't mean, taking the pressure off and drawing the relationship closer together.

Another gift of patience is that it allows your partner to feel cherished and important. You are giving the message that they matter to you and that you are willing to love and be supportive. It nourishes the relationship and increases the level of trust and understanding. This means that when times are hectic, which is inevitable, there is an emotional reservoir of strength and empathy that can be drawn upon.

The irony of patience is that although it can seem to take more time and effort, it is a great time saver. By being patient you give your partner the opportunity to communicate fully. This means that you won't have to keep going back over old ground. Once something is expressed and heard, resolution is reached, enabling you to move forward with confidence.

Another aspect of patience is to give your partner space. We all communicate and process information at different speeds. Typically, when you confront your partner, or when you want to have a serious discussion, it can be difficult to articulate your position and to embrace their position without becoming at least slightly defensive. Giving space is not necessarily something you have to do in a physical sense. It is a decision to have unconditional regard for your partner and to allow them the room to make mistakes, to change opinions and to see things differently. Commit to the path of least resistance in your relationship by practising patience and opening a door to deeper communication.

The truth shall set you free

The old saying, 'The truth shall set you free' has great wisdom in it, although it's worth mentioning that at first it might piss you off! I have had many debates about telling the truth and being honest in a relationship and have concluded that however challenging, it is the best policy. The opportunity that it brings enables you to choose the next step in a relationship from a position of strength and clarity rather than of fear or confusion.

The following story illustrates what can happen if nobody is willing to tell the truth:

It was a hot day and the Wright family was lying by a pool in a rented villa on their summer holiday. This year they had invited their friends the Jones family to join them. They were happily playing backgammon and reading gripping thrillers when Mr Jones suggested that they should go and visit the local town. Mr Wright thought, 'What! Go to the shops, in this heat, when we're all happy here, what madness!'

But Mrs Wright said, 'Sounds like a great idea. I'd love to go.' Mrs Jones then put down her book and also exclaimed that she would also be happy to go. Mr Wright felt unable to say what he really wanted, so turned to the children, who were enjoying the pool, hoping that they might object. However, his hopes were destroyed. 'Of course we want to go to the shops,' they said.

The expedition fulfilled Mr Wright's worst expectations. It was hot and humid, the shops were full of nothing in particular, the children got on each other's nerves and the café they stopped in served awful food. Four hours later they arrived home, hot and bothered.

Later that evening Mr Jones eventually admitted that he would rather have stayed by the pool in the first place but was concerned that the others would be bored. Mrs Wright said that she had agreed with him only to be sociable and keep the others happy. Mr Wright couldn't believe what he was hearing. The final blow was when the children piped up that they would have had to be crazy to want to go out on a day like that but felt they had to please their parents.

Mr Wright reflected: Here we were, two reasonable families who, by our own accord, had left the peace and quiet of the villa to go shopping in the heat of the day, and had eaten at a unappealing café, when none of us had really wanted to go. How different it would have been if we'd been honest in the first place.

Do you relate to this scene? Are there areas in your life where you are not telling the truth and doing the opposite of what you really want? The fear of being honest can be so strong that it prevents us from following our heart and soul.

I have seen many relationships destroyed by a lack of true communication, where roles are played and feelings remain unexpressed. I once worked with a couple who were willing to communicate truthfully, having got 'stuck' in their relationship. They had been together for several years, in which time they had grown apart and lived quite separate lives. The combination of long working hours and travel had taken its toll and meant that often they didn't see each other for days at a time. They had reached make or break – either they were to come together or to separate but they were unsure which avenue to take.

The starting point was to express the truth for each of them before any decision could be reached. We established clear boundaries for communication to take place. They would both have the opportunity to be honest without interruption or comments. The intention of the communication was to air feelings for the purpose of gaining greater clarity and insight. Sarah spoke first and initially expressed her fears of being ridiculed, of hurting Mike's feelings, of having to change her life, of losing the relationship, of staying 'stuck' and of things getting worse. She continued by disclosing that she felt the relationship had lost its spark, that she gained most of her companionship and support from her friends and that she believed it was over.

She couldn't imagine rekindling the love that brought them together. She talked about the sadness she felt that the relationship had reached this state. It reminded her of her parents' marriage and she didn't want to go down the same road.

Mike listened carefully. Once Sarah had concluded we paused and then he expressed his truth. He felt angry that they had neglected the relationship. He put it down to the pressure of working to maintain a high standard of living, which gave them little time to spend together. He experienced Sarah cutting him out of her life and felt he became more withdrawn as a result. He found solace in his work because it didn't disturb his equilibrium. He felt frustrated; his needs were unmet and he disclosed that he had been tempted to leave but wanted to give the relationship one last chance.

Following their willingness to be honest you could feel the sense of relief in the room. Although it had been challenging they both agreed that it was a weight off their shoulders and that they could now begin anew. I encouraged them not to make any major decisions in the next week but to continue the process of expressing and hearing each other's truth.

You do not need to attend a coaching session to start this process, although it can be helpful if a lot of water has passed under the bridge. A useful communication tool to help clarify feelings in a relationship is to write letters. These give you space to express your concerns, preferences, desires, or potential solutions without having to confront your partner face-to-face. This can take the sting out of a potentially difficult situation because it gives you the chance to think about your position and describe it slowly. Your partner is able to read it in their time, reflect upon it and respond away from the heat of the moment.

If you feel overwhelmed by the amount you want to say, a good move is to write a letter but not to send it; this letter is simply for your own personal release. It gives you the opportunity to express yourself without worrying about the response. The act of doing this enables you to let go of feelings and to see your relationship in a clearer light. You can then write a further version without the emotional weight that you were originally carrying and give it to your partner.

I have found that the most useful times to write these letters are either when I've had an argument with Veronica or when I want to say how much I love her. Sometimes it's difficult to resolve a conflict due to the emotional intensity. I have learned that the wisest thing can be to walk away and to revisit it when things have calmed down. During the cooling-off period is the best time to write. It brings things back into perspective and reminds you what is truly important, which is usually not what you were arguing about. Leaving this note for your partner to read shows that you care and it is often helpful for them to see your position stated in black and white. As long as it's written with genuine love and respect, it's hard to imagine that it wouldn't be well received; and letting your partner know how much you love and care about them through the written word is a wonderful way to touch their heart.

Whether you decide to talk or to write letters your commitment to M.O.T.s (moments of truth) nourishes and supports your relationship. A motto I once heard was, 'Tell the truth faster'. This ensures that your relationship is based on honesty, promoting trust and respect – essential qualities for an intelligent relationship.

6

Love & Intimacy

THE PRINCIPLE OF SEXUALITY

A very handsome man walks into a room. He is introduced to a beautiful woman. You can feel the electricity between them, a current rippling with sexual energy. Within minutes they have escaped to another room and fulfilled their passionate desire. One hour later he meets another stunning woman. The intensity is unbearable. They make love. It's hard to believe but the last you see of him he is in the arms of yet another gorgeous woman, with no strings attached, no pain, no mess and no problems. His name – Bond, James Bond.

Have you tried to live up to the images of the perfect sexual experience that we have been bombarded with? It's not surprising that we have a distorted idea about sexuality with the media portraying ideal bodies, multiple orgasms and insatiable passion on tap 24 hours a day. All this can leave us with feelings of sexual inadequacy, and unless we redefine our attitude to our own sexuality it remains unfulfilled.

The principle of sexuality looks at the importance of creating emotional intimacy within a relationship. So often we just go for the physical workout of sex which, although it feels great, if there is no emotional connection prevents us from being fulfilled. This chapter also covers the value of clear communication, being able to talk openly about sexuality and our sexual feelings in order to create greater intimacy. It embraces the idea that sex should be fun and is not to be taken too seriously. Ultimately, sexuality is an expression of love, of which having sex is one aspect. In truth sexuality is at the heart of many areas of life, stimulating creativity, fun, laughter and joy if we let it.

An expression of love

Woody Allen once said that 'sex without love is an empty experience, but as empty experiences go, it's pretty good'. In modern living sex without love has become a norm. Men tend to believe that they can satisfy their sexual needs without becoming emotionally involved and women may use it to fill a gap in their lives or a craving for love. This behaviour can be hard to give up when we want to create a fulfilled intimate relationship. There is no such thing as casual sex. All sexual activity involves an exchange of energy and although you can become an expert in cutting yourself off from your feelings, this does not mean that it has no impact.

The experience of sex in a monogamous relationship is different from that in the dating game. It's not better or worse, but unless we redefine it our expectations can take us off track. I often hear couples saying how they are too tired to have sex; the demands of work or a family take over. Men feel rejected when a woman isn't in the mood for sex and women don't feel romanced and understood in the relationship. If we don't resolve these dilemmas the drive to meet our sexual needs may result in secret fantasies which prevent us from being present with our partner, and also create the possibility of having affairs. The commitment to making sex an expression of love removes it from the purely physical aspect of lovemaking and brings it into your communication and romance.

I worked with a client who was obsessed with sex. Steven was in a relationship but felt that his partner did not satisfy him sexually. Subsequently he became consumed by the need to attract other women. He had affairs and became a compulsive liar, only seeking help when he realised how damaging it was. When we traced the source of his behaviour he recognised that it was influenced by his father who had had affairs during his marriage. Although Steven saw how detrimental it was to his parents' relationship, he felt unable to break the pattern for himself.

As with any addictive behaviour, the starting point to ending it is to admit that we are powerless and that our lives have become unmanageable. This is the first step recommended by twelve step programmes such as Alcoholics Anonymous and the sex addiction programme, Sex and Love Anonymous. Steven entered this programme to receive the necessary group support and structure to help him stop having affairs. He went through a testing period as he weaned himself off his obsession. He began communicating with his partner in an entirely new way and committed to taking responsibility for his feelings and telling her if he felt unsatisfied. He decided to learn how to make sex a truly meaningful and fulfilling experience by considering his partner's needs for romance, understanding and intimacy. This allowed sex to become an expression of love in his relationship and filled the void that had previously been there.

The choice to make sex an expression of love is what transforms it from being sometimes a duty or a performance into an extraordinary experience. You open your relationship to new levels of intimacy and union that include feelings of being without boundaries or limitations. One of the main reasons why you may not have had this experience can be a fear of its power. You may reach an intimacy threshold, when a certain amount of intimacy is reached; it is uncomfortable for your partner to come any closer. At this point there can be a tendency to sabotage the intimacy that you have and to revert to more familiar territory.

To read intimacy as *into-me-see* gives an understanding of why we might resist it. It is a deeply personal experience that requires the two people within a relationship to be connected on physical, emotional, mental and spiritual levels. Unless we nurture and develop each one of these different aspects of who we are, our intimacy threshold may surface by one partner generally pulling away and the other feeling more needy. Recognising these traits enables you to choose to go beyond your intimacy threshold and focus on deepening your connection.

Developing your sexuality as an expression of love nurtures your connection at each of the four levels. It deepens your experience of sex by opening communication, it strengthens your emotional connection by giving greater affection, it increases your mental connection by creating new possibilities and it heightens your spiritual connection through unconditional love.

Allowing intimacy to grow also removes concerns such as performance anxiety, body image and lethargy, and connects you with the life force, known as 'chi', 'prana', or 'kundalini'. This form of sexual union and intimacy, commonly called tantra, is perceived as a path to bliss in certain cultures. It unleashes the tremendous power of love and sexual energy combined, which can transform your relationship into a continuous source of joy and passion.

We have become dominated by the orgasm, the peak experience, which often leaves a man feeling drained and which women can find difficult to experience. Letting your lovemaking be a spiritual and sacred act builds energy and removes the urge to make the orgasm the ultimate goal. This energy keeps sexual interest alive and ensures that every physical encounter and gesture within the relationship is a meaningful experience and can lead you to the divinity of your relationship, which is at the very centre of its existence.

Decide to deepen your experience of sexuality. Ask yourself: *'how can I make my sexuality an expression of love?'* Sharing this with your partner will demonstrate your willingness to enhance your partnership and allow your intimacy to grow.

Sexual healing

I blame my mother for my poor sex life. All she told me was 'the man goes on top and the woman underneath'. For three years my husband and I slept in bunk beds.

Joan Rivers

The theme of sexual healing involves letting go of sexual memories, any fears around sexuality, past limiting beliefs and negative expectations. We have all had different sexual conditioning, which influences our current reality. Some of the main elements involved are feelings of shame and embarrassment, a sense of unworthiness, poor self-image and performance anxiety caused by a variety of factors including parental, educational, religious and previous relationship experience. It's surprising how many people you can take to bed with you until you free and release yourself from your sexual past. A parent may spring to mind, a teacher's voice might be heard, religious messages can dominate, or an ex-lover could surface, all of which can detract from your relationship.

In my Relationship Intelligence Seminar one of the most amusing sessions is the one focused on transforming our past beliefs about sexuality. An exercise participants do is to write down their unhelpful beliefs about sex. This allows them to discover the decisions that they have made and to re-evaluate their position. Much laughter is created as people share what they have written. Some of the limiting beliefs that women have spoken about include:

- You don't get what you want.
- There is not enough romance.
- Men don't understand me.
- I can't get my needs met.
- Men just expect it.
- I'm not happy with the way I look.
- Body issues get in the way.
- My body is not toned enough. It's too fat.
- PMT.
- I'm too tired. I haven't got the energy.
- When I want it he doesn't, and when he wants it I don't.
- I don't get enough of it.
- It's boring.
- It's not fulfilling.
- It leaves me empty.

Some of the beliefs that men have written about are:

- It's expensive; dinners, champagne, gifts.
- Foreplay takes too long.

- ◆ Performance anxiety – will I please her?
- ◆ Women reject my advances.
- ◆ I have to do all the work.
- ◆ I don't get what I want.
- ◆ I don't get enough of it.
- ◆ Sex is time-consuming.
- ◆ I'm not masculine enough.
- ◆ Sex in a long-term relationship is not passionate or wild enough.
- ◆ I can't be bothered.
- ◆ Making love gets too intimate.
- ◆ Women are not enthusiastic enough.

It is not surprising that by holding on to these types of beliefs we do not experience the sexual enjoyment that we would like. Often we continue to hold on to our beliefs because we feel hurt or resentful at not having our needs met. We place conditions between our partner and ourselves, silently stating, 'I'll let go of my position if you meet my needs.' Our needs will not be met until we are willing to transform our perception. You cannot change your previous experiences but you can change the decisions that you made about them. By doing so you soften your position, adopt a more flexible outlook and open yourself to a new and improved sex life.

One lady who attended a workshop wrote to me several weeks later with a happy report of her changing fortunes. She had been married for several years and their sex life had become extremely unfulfilling. When she first wrote down her beliefs, she realised that she was holding her husband responsible for her experiences. Upon reflection she decided to be willing to see him differently. She entertained the possibility that he was a caring, considerate lover who enjoyed meeting her sexual needs. She focused on the time and energy that they gave to sexual intimacy and committed to appreciating her own body. She found that it threw a new light on how she approached sex. She no longer looked for evidence to prove that her husband couldn't meet her needs. She relaxed and allowed him to become closer to her. She said that he was delighted. They discussed her changed outlook, which then enabled him to reflect on his viewpoint and make changes for the better.

Once you have become aware of your current attitude about sex, if it doesn't support you then make the decision to change. As there will be a time gap between changing your mind and having a different experience, be patient and trust in the outcome. The following are some new beliefs that people have adopted:

- My partner and I can both get what we want sexually.
- We seek to understand each other and communicate clearly before, during and after sex.
- I now take responsibility for meeting my sexual needs.
- My body is a source of pleasure and being sexual is a source of pleasure and enjoyment.
- Sex is fun.
- Sexual intimacy is a gift.

Developing a new attitude heals unresolved sexual issues. By taking personal responsibility and being accountable for your present choices, it allows you to let go of the past and to make peace with your sexuality. Your willingness to work through issues as they arise provides the necessary strength for your relationship to thrive. I have seen many relationships on the verge of breaking down due to unresolved sexual matters; once healed a new beginning is possible.

Another element in sexual dilemmas is fear, in particular the fear of repeating painful past experiences. If you have suffered previous upset it is understandable that you might be apprehensive and lack trust; therefore it is important to be compassionate and gentle with yourself as you move through fear. Since our natural response to fear is fight or flight, you might find yourself either confronting your partner or avoiding them if fear surfaces. The key to healing this dynamic is to be able to communicate your fears in a safe and supportive way. Common fears include: vulnerability and feeling exposed, loss, embarrassment, shame, making mistakes, physical pain and not being satisfied.

I had a male client who suffered from performance anxiety. It had reached the stage where John was unable to sustain an erection during lovemaking. Although his partner showed understanding he felt ashamed and lost interest in sex. We looked at the origins of the problem, in particular what he had told himself to hide or cover up his sense of failure. John traced it back to an early sexual experience when he had not been able to perform with a girlfriend. He had told himself that he was no good as a man and that women would not find him attractive. This dented his confidence and kept the anxiety alive. I pointed out that what he had told himself was simply an interpretation of what happened, which he could change.

John recognised that just because he had a difficulty with sustaining an erection it did not mean that he was no good as a man. In fact his courage to be in a relationship and share it with his partner meant that he was going beyond the macho image of a man and could develop intimacy on all levels of the relation- ship. By shifting his focus it took the pressure off having to per- form and they could explore different aspects of their sexuality.

Developing a greater awareness of your fears and having the confidence to disclose them lessens their impact. Once you are able to name a fear it no longer troubles you unconsciously. If the fear arises in the future you are able to identify it and to put it in perspective. The greatest support that your partner can give is to hear you and not try to heal you. They are simply fears that you need to express in order to be able to see them in a different light.

Healing negative expectations is a similar process. To what- ever extent you or your partner suppress your sexuality to meet expectations, the attraction will fade. For example if you expect your partner to want to make love every day you'll probably be in for a shock. Or if you try and alter, fix, or improve your partner, you are sending them the message that they are not okay. Under these conditions, passion dies. Removing expecta- tions frees sexuality and allows your relationship to be based on what is true to you both.

Think about how you could benefit from sexual healing. Do you have any limiting beliefs or fears that hold you back? Do you have some expectations that cause love to diminish? If so, your commitment to your own healing will transform your experience of the relationship.

Sexual intimacy

Have you ever experienced the dance that can occur in a relationship with the old story of, 'when I want you, you don't want me; when I back off and don't want you, you then want me'? If so, you will appreciate how it blocks sexual intimacy. What motivates us to play this push/pull game is a dynamic that often relates back to childhood. Whilst growing up it is common to want special attention from the parent of the opposite sex. Children harmlessly say, 'when I grow up I'm going to marry my mother/father'. As it is not appropriate to have a sexual relationship with a parent, unconscious decisions can be made that either they are not attractive to the person they want, or that they are not attracted to the person who wants them.

As an adult this may create a pattern of being attracted to someone when they are unavailable physically, emotionally or psychologically or vice versa. For example, you might find that you want your partner when they are busy with a work project, but when they finish it you lose interest. It may mean that your relationship is long-distance and that you can only handle so much time together or that you are in a relationship but secretly wanting to be with someone else. Another way this pattern can reveal itself is to have sexual fantasies and make comparisons, which prevent you from being sexually intimate with your partner and can lead to feelings of guilt and shame. Your ability to recognise and understand this dynamic allows you to discuss it in an open and constructive way.

I saw a couple called Nigel and Louise whose relationship was dominated by this pattern. They met whilst they were both unavailable and had a hidden affair until they ended the relationships they were in. They agreed to move in together, but when it came to the day Nigel had cold feet and called it off. The following day he was on the phone to Louise wanting it to go ahead. Eventually they did move in together, and at that point their sex life dried up. Louise found herself thinking about past relationships and Nigel started looking at other women. It was at this point that they came to see me. When I pointed out the push/pull game that they were caught in it was a relief to them both. They related to it fully and were relieved by the fact that they were not unique in being caught in this dynamic.

I asked them each to make a note whenever they reached an intimacy threshold and to show how it affected the relationship. They began to see a pattern emerging: as soon as the relationship appeared too familiar one or both would slip into the dynamic. It caused them to go into their own separate worlds and to close off from each other. In this space of separation neither could imagine the relationship working and both conjured up plans to leave. Luckily one of them would stay sane enough to see what was happening; they were continuing a habit that they had played in many previous relationships, but which they both wished to leave behind.

As Nigel continued to look at other women I suggested that he follow the 'three-second rule', to look at women to whom he was attracted for three seconds and then to look away. This forces you to become conscious that you are caught in the habit of being attracted to the unavailable and enables you to make the conscious choice to stop it. Although flirting is often socially acceptable, it is potentially damaging to the sexual intimacy of a relationship if continued over time.

I suggested to Louise that she make a list of the men that she had been in past relationships with, and by each name write a statement to bring closure to the attraction. For example to her previous lover, she wrote, 'Gary, although I enjoyed our time together, it is no longer appropriate for me to fantasise about you, to imagine what it would be like to be with you and to compare Nigel to you. I wish you all the best for the future and lovingly let you go.' Doing this symbolised her intention to close each chapter of her past relationships and finally to move on.

I encouraged them to share these moments of distraction when they surfaced in order to bring them into the open and to have no secrets between themselves. Since it is often the secrecy of a fantasy or of being attracted to an unavailable person that keeps the pattern in place, talking about it with your partner, with the intention of creating love and understanding, removes the veil of secrecy and hence the pull of the attraction.

It is important not to jump to conclusions from this type of behaviour. It is quite natural to continue to find other people attractive, or have fantasies when in a committed relationship, however the quicker you let it go, the quicker you can be fully intimate with your partner again. Be aware that continuing push/pull games is exhausting and prevents you from enjoying the closeness and growth that clearing this pattern can bring.

Let's talk about it

I wasn't kissing your daughter, sir – I was just whispering in her mouth.

Chico Marx

Do you remember the following scene in *When Harry Met Sally*? They are sitting in a café and Harry (Billy Crystal) is saying that he thinks women have an okay time with him sexually. Sally (Meg Ryan) questions him on his assumption and asks him how he knows. He replies that he just knows but gets quite concerned that she might be saying that they fake orgasm with him. She says it's quite possible since most women at one time or another have faked it. Harry claims that they haven't faked it with him. Sally then goes on to perform a perfect rendition of an orgasm. Harry is taken aback, whilst at another table a lady who has been watching orders whatever she's having to eat.

It's easy to assume that you know what your partner wants and enjoys without having fully communicated about it. In fact talking about sex can be a sensitive and emotive subject. How comfortable are you when talking about it with your partner? Does talking about sex make you feel embarrassed, defensive or insecure? There are five main factors that can affect communicating about sex in a relationship. They are:

1. If sex was considered a taboo subject in your family, then you probably grew up with the belief that it was not acceptable to communicate about it.
2. If you experienced religious conditioning about sex, including receiving messages such as sex is wrong, bad or sinful it can colour your outlook and give rise to feelings of guilt and shame.
3. If your sex education was inadequate and conveyed in an atmosphere of embarrassment, it may contribute to a sense of discomfort regarding sex and communication.
4. If you have had a painful past experience communicating about sex in a relationship, it might cause you to withdraw from communicating with your current partner.
5. The current social climate makes people ashamed to admit to any perceived sexual failures or inadequacies.

Whatever your past experience, learning to talk freely and spontaneously about sex brings you closer together. I worked with a couple who had been together for several years. Initially they had enjoyed an active sex life, full of passion, romance and excitement. During the two years before coming to see me their sex life had gone dead. The mutual attraction seemed to have disappeared and they were both wondering what had gone wrong. When we started to diagnose the situation it became apparent that neither of them felt comfortable talking about sex. Paul had grown up in a Catholic family where sex was never discussed and he was warned never to bring a girlfriend in to the house. Jane's parents divorced when she was a young girl, her mother never remarried, and as a result she didn't have an example of a healthy, loving relationship.

They agreed to disclose their feelings to each other and to listen with acceptance. Paul said how he felt rejected by Jane, as she no longer reciprocated his sexual advances. The consequence was that he channelled more of his energy into his work and hobbies and rarely thought about sex. Jane revealed that she didn't feel Paul understood her as he no longer paid attention to her opinions. Ironically, she spent more time with her own friends discussing how men don't understand women's needs than trying to resolve things directly with Paul. I suggested that they continue to discuss their feelings with the intention of resuming sexual relations. It required patience and compassion to unlock their hearts again to each other, but as they continued to do so sexual feelings returned.

Reflect on your current or most recent relationship. Did you find that it went sexually dead at any particular stage? If so, what helped you resume the sexual intimacy? Being willing to communicate releases blocks and frees you to be sexual again. In essence sex is a form of intimate communication, an exchange of energy that responds to the relationship as a whole. If there are various elements in your relationship that are unclear, they will have a direct impact on your sexual interaction.

I liken sexual energy to a radio frequency and the relationship to the receiver. If there are blocks in communication these prevent the frequency from reaching the receiver clearly. The receiver might work perfectly well but without a clear frequency it is unable to play. Just because your relationship has gone sexually dead does not mean that there is anything wrong with it; to communicate clears the frequency and allows the relationship to restore its sexual activity.

The key to talking about sex in your relationship is to be compassionate and to seek to understand your partner. As it is a delicate area where people may feel quite threatened, extending unconditional acceptance provides a safe context for your partner to express himself or herself. Choose an appropriate time when you have some space away from your normal routine. Make sure that you have a mutual agreement to talk about sex and your sexual feelings. Set the intention to clear past feelings and resolve issues in order to be fully present now. Give each other time to clarify your thoughts and don't jump to conclusions. Since your self-esteem is often linked to your sexuality it is easy to take things personally and to feel hurt or betrayed by what your partner says. It is crucial to remember that the purpose of the communication is to release the past, not to reinforce it.

Another ingredient in a healthy sex life is to know that you deserve to have your sexual needs met. Unless you feel that it is your intrinsic right as a human being you might feel guilty when you start to communicate, which can cause a blockage to asking for what you want. Don't be under the illusion that you are supposed to know intuitively exactly what your partner likes and wants, and to be able to meet their needs without them being discussed. One of the greatest joys in sex is being able to share your needs with your partner and to enable him or her to meet them. It is an expression of true intimacy and a commitment to your love for each other.

Lighten up!

Sex should be fun. The challenge in a relationship is to keep it fun. We can take it so seriously that we forget to enjoy ourselves. We can make it a performance that we think we're going to get judged for. We can turn it into a power game and fight to see who wins. We can use it as a compensation for troubles in other areas. Ideally sex is simply an opportunity to share intimacy, affection, love and passion. It is a way to communicate love and attraction for your partner and have fun together.

To start the process of lightening up your sex life, write down a description of your ideal sexual experience. Let your imagination take over. Make sure that you include the type of environment, atmosphere, emotional feeling, mental connection, physical expression and spiritual dimension that you want. Allow it to have the romance, passion, sensuality, joy and laughter that you desire. Share this scenario with your partner. It can add a new dimension to your sex life, igniting it if it has gone dead or enhancing it if it's active. Remind yourself that it is innocent to enjoy your sexuality and that the decision to lighten up about it keeps it alive.

Having focused on your ideal experience it's important to

remember that in our busy lives you do not need to have all the right conditions in place to enjoy your sexuality. Often you need to allow yourself to be spontaneous and not to let other tasks distract you. If you have a routine of coming home, making dinner and watching television, change it. Decide to be sexual before you retire to bed. Being sexually active does not necessarily mean that you have to make love each time. Allowing sexual energy to build between you by being affectionate and playful enriches the relationship. Even engaging in five or ten minutes of sexual activity can help you to break out of the habit of keeping busy and postponing something as enjoyable and meaningful as sex.

Eddie and Kelly are fun to be with. They have a great capacity for laughter, playfulness and joy in their life. When I asked them what nourishes and enhances their relationship they replied great communication, great sex and lots of love. When they first met they were both in recovery from previous break-ups. Feeling vulnerable, they developed a friendship in which they were able to tell each other things that previously they had kept hidden in their relationships. It had led to a level of intimacy that allowed them to be true to themselves. Over a period of time they admitted their attraction to each other and became sexually involved.

They discovered that the level of friendship they had developed helped them to handle the increased intensity of a sexual relationship. They stayed playful and learned to laugh about many of the issues that had hindered their past relationships.

Remember that having great sexual experiences strengthens your relationship. It is not just a symptom of a successful relationship but a major factor in creating one. Enjoying sexuality fills your heart with love and nourishes your connection.

7

Opportunity Knocks

THE PRINCIPLE OF CHANGE

We live in a changing world. In fact the rate of change today has accelerated beyond belief. A global economy, the World Wide Web, short-term contracts, flexi-hours, hot-desking and self-employment are some of the changes that have transformed our working lives. Technological advancements mean that we live a mobile existence and have radically changed our social habits. Changes in family structures and social values have also created a new outlook and approach to life. As human beings we are faced with the prospect of having to adapt to these changes. Sometimes this can be difficult as we may dislike, disagree with or resist the change, and find it uncomfortable to embrace what is new.

Relationships are no exception to the process of change. You will notice that a relationship goes through different stages of change, whether you like it or not. This can come as a great relief if you are stuck in an unhappy period, but it might not be so welcome if you're enjoying a romantic time.

As creatures of habit we cling to what is familiar. Even if something is not working or detrimental to our well-being we might still resist change. If battered children are removed from their parents, the very source of their agony, they reach out to go back. People return to destructive relationships over and over, even after agreeing to leave. Alcoholics have one more drink when they know the slippery path that it entails. Often we are our own worst enemies when it comes to managing change. However, by understanding the stages of change that occur in a relationship, and by creating strategies to rise to the challenge, we can welcome change as an important aspect of our growth and development.

Change is inevitable

Wouldn't it be great if a relationship came in a package that included: undying love, unlimited passion, complete understanding, total harmony and large amounts of happiness, with a money-back guarantee? Unfortunately, no matter how close together we are the only guarantee in a relationship is change. It will evolve, grow and develop. Understanding and accepting the inevitability of change adds to the richness and quality of our experience.

There are five main stages in a relationship which, when recognised and accepted, can help you to grow together apart. They are:

1. The romantic stage: the shelf life can be as little as two months
2. The disillusionment stage: can last up to two years
3. The misery stage: can last up to 30 years
4. The awakening stage: when the couple accepts personal responsibility and accountability for their choices
5. The mutual respect stage: the intelligent relationship.

We have been raised on stories of romance that colour our perception of relationships. For us as children, fairy tales such as Sleeping Beauty, Rapunzel and Cinderella painted pictures of the damsel in distress rescued by the knight in shining armour who then both go on to live happily ever after. For adults, movies like *Breakfast At Tiffany's*, *Love Story* and *Pretty Woman* ensure that the romantic dream stays alive. We spend large amounts of money on romantic pursuits including exotic holidays, weekend breaks, candlelit dinners, items of clothing and beautiful gifts to woo our partners and keep the magic alive.

The romantic stage in a relationship, also known as the honeymoon or wonder period, is characterised by a whirlwind of excitement and passion. You perceive your partner as being able to do no wrong. If they are late for a very important date you love the anticipation. If they make mistakes you are charmed by their humanness and if they have a bad hair day you enjoy comforting them. Your life becomes dominated by the relationship, you catch yourself thinking about it for most of the day and it is difficult to concentrate on normal activities. You dress well, become spontaneous in your choice of activities and have unlimited energy. It's great stuff – and it will change.

It is unrealistic to expect the romantic stage to last forever. However, the change in the intensity of emotion does not mean that your relationship is invalid or that the romance has gone out of it. This understanding ensures that your relationship can grow and mature without spending too much time in the disillusionment stage. This stage is characterised by your partner falling off his or her pedestal and seemingly becoming just like everyone else. Suddenly the traits that were so appealing become annoyances, and you may begin to question the validity of the relationship. It is comparable to an adolescent realising that parents are only human and not perfect. This may come as a shock and be accompanied with feelings of betrayal and mistrust. However, in order for a young person to become autonomous it's important that they go through this period and let go of the image of the infallible parent.

I remember passing through the disillusionment stage with Veronica. When we first met I loved her sense of possibility and optimism. She had a relaxed attitude that was refreshing and fun. When the initial romance changed I began to react differently. I looked for reasons to knock her approach and adopted a role of superiority, which I masked as being realistic. It is vital in this stage to accept responsibility for your position and to be aware when you project your own thinking on to your partner. By accepting responsibility I saw that Veronica hadn't changed, my perception had. Being able to catch this dynamic helped me to see the disillusionment stage for what it really is – just an illusion. It is not real or permanent. Your willingness to see beyond the apparent loss of magic supports the natural transition during the early life of a relationship.

The next stage, the misery stage, also known as the dead zone, is the most difficult period of a relationship. Unfortunately, some relationships spend most of their time here if neither person is prepared to accept responsibility and become open to new possibilities. This stage is characterised by people feeling victimised by the relationship, blaming it for any unhappiness, or failure they have and kidding themselves that if it wasn't for the relationship they'd be happy, successful and free.

The main reason a relationship hits this stage is because 'roles' are played, which are behavioural patterns formed as a compensation for feeling unworthy and not good enough. They prevent you from being your authentic self, causing you to limit your self-expression and vitality. Some classic roles include:

◈ **The victim**. Victims tell themselves: 'poor me, life's so hard, everybody's out to get me, why does it always happen to me, I can't get what I want'. Victims feel powerless and that there is nothing they can do to make things better. They hold back communication whilst silently blaming their partner for their woes. Victims are dependent on their partner, believing that they cannot function without them.

◈ **The control freak**. A stickler for detail, control freaks dominate the relationship through manipulation. They become angry easily and cause their partner to feel guilty or afraid. They blame their partner if anything is not to their liking. Control freaks exercise independence to the extreme, pretending that they do not need their partner.

◈ **The pleaser**. Pleasers play the role of the 'good' partner, but it leaves a sickly taste in the mouth because it is inauthentic. They bow to their partner's whims without standing up for their own beliefs. Pleasers might spend a lifetime trying to make their partner happy, however they never achieve the desired result because they lose respect due to their weak behaviour.

◆ **The wounded**. Like the victims, the wounded want to be rescued. They carry a broken wing, which can never be repaired. They cry out for help but no aid is ever good enough. They get their partner to feel sorry for them, but it's a form of manipulation.

We are all susceptible to playing these roles at one time or another. When we do, we fail to bring the essence of ourselves to the relationship. It's comparable to wearing a mask behind which lies the real you. The relationship goes dead because it's no longer truly alive. Tell-tale signs of being in the misery stage are:

◆ You're miserable, feeling bored, trapped, and irritable.
◆ You fantasise about leaving the relationship, yet you know it's not the solution.
◆ You resign yourself to the status quo.
◆ You pretend that everything's *fine* (an acronym for Fucked up, Insecure, Neurotic and Emotional.)
◆ There is low energy, no spontaneity and fun.
◆ The passion has died.
◆ A distinct lack of laughter.
◆ Sex is routine, if at all.
◆ A desire to give up on relationships altogether.

If you find yourself in the misery stage I encourage you to give up misery before giving up on the relationship. Tell yourself that *this too will pass* if you're having a hard time. Remind yourself that *change is inevitable*. Be honest about what's happening and how you're feeling. Accepting responsibility for your experience and committing to seeing things differently enables you to ride the waves if they come crashing towards you.

At this time people often question whether a relationship is right or not. A good indicator is that if you have accepted responsibility, stopped playing roles, been honest about your feelings, and are still finding yourself stuck in the misery stage, it might be that your relationship does not have a future in its current form. Therefore the most loving thing could be to let it go. This requires faith, keeping a flexible outlook, and staying honest about how you feel. Any separation is painful, but if you have a clear enough understanding of why it is happening, you can handle any outcome. To end a relationship is not a failure. There are many lessons to be learnt and gifts to be received in each encounter, which support our journey through life.

Committing to the process of accepting responsibility and being accountable for your choices is an aspect of the awakening stage. This is characterised by moments of realisation and joy. You experience miracles in your relationship. A miracle is an unpredictable shift in perception; it is seeing something differently without necessarily knowing how you came to view it in a new light. For example, one moment you might see your partner as your enemy, the next your closest friend; or you may start perceiving them as holding you back and the next as helping you to break through limits. The awakening stage requires flexibility, trust and a willingness to move forward. This allows you to draw on reservoirs of strength that are not available to you when preoccupied by the roles, power struggles and game playing which dominate the misery stage.

I have seen many couples' relationships transformed during the awakening stage. Some close friends experienced a break-through in their marriage as a result of making new choices. They were in continual conflict over their work/life balance. Richard worked all hours running his successful computer company. Catherine became increasingly frustrated, feeling that he saw his work as more important than their marriage, and she kept threatening to leave. Each time she did Richard came running back and they resumed a relative equilibrium. This continued until the old problem flared up again and they went through the same cycle. One weekend they went away to face the situation undisturbed. They spent time in silence together, they listened to each other with respect and love, they disclosed their greatest fears and deepest hurts and they revealed their dreams and hopes. Upon returning to their regular lives they had a renewed commitment to keeping a healthy balance between managing their work and life together.

When I asked them what their biggest realisation had been, they replied that it was to live fully now and not so many years in the future. They shared with me a piece of wisdom that had touched them: 'If you take care of each instant, you will take care of all time. There is only one time when it is essential to awaken. That time is now.' They became good examples of how taking care of each instant takes care of all time. They stopped worrying about what was going to happen and placed their full attention on the next step in front of them. They began to experience a truly synergistic relationship, co-operating and working in true partnership and supporting each other when challenges arose. It was a joy to see and they continue to inspire me by continually strengthening their relationship.

Moving through the awakening stage brings you to the stage of mutual respect. This is characterised by a true sense of companionship, unconditional love and pure joy. Your choices are win/win; you enjoy empathetic communication and harmony together, and a healthy sex life. To have mutual respect is at the heart of a successful relationship. It brings dignity and grace, preventing you from taking your partner for granted and not appreciating all the gifts that they bring. I often see and hear people communicating with their supposed loved one in a way that they would never dream of doing with a friend or colleague. It is not okay to let your standards drop. The choice to respect your partner brings out the best in them and allows you to reap the benefits of your commitment to having an extraordinary relationship.

Rising to the challenge

Richard and Jerry were having a roller coaster period in their marriage. They had been together for over ten years and had three young children. Things began to change when Richard took on a new project at work demanding great commitment, focus and energy. This had an impact on their relationship. Their time together was tense, both over-reacting to the complications of everyday life and blaming each other for their stress. When they came to see me it had reached a breaking point.

Having listened to their situation I asked them to look at what the experience of change meant to them. Jerry disclosed that she had watched her parents' marriage suffer when her father had been involved with all-consuming work projects. As a result she felt threatened by their changing circumstances and wanted to revert to the status quo. On the other hand Richard had observed his father failing to achieve at work, and had experienced great concern at the prospect of not succeeding in his own career. Therefore he welcomed the change and wanted it to continue. Sharing these two points of view enabled them to understand that although they were experiencing the same situation in their life, their interpretation of it was at the heart of the conflict. They had differing positions and could either rise to the challenge of change, or resist it and suffer.

I suggested that having reflected on their interpretation of change, they could see it as an opportunity. Since change is inevitable, the sooner we can welcome it the more effectively we can handle it. Jerry chose to accept the change as a natural part of life and to embrace it as an opportunity to strengthen and deepen their relationship. Richard considered the possibility that the changes at work were an indication that he was already succeeding and saw that he could relax more and therefore prevent them from damaging his family. Shifting their outlook towards change enabled them to work with it rather than against it. They understood that a relationship is constantly evolving and that without movement it becomes stagnant. They committed to being flexible in response to change, which transformed the way they dealt with it.

How do you perceive change? Do you see it as an opportunity or a threat? Do you rise to the challenge? Do you welcome or resist it? Reflecting on the major changes that you have experienced in relationships and your responses to them enables you to gain greater clarity and to make new choices. I used to feel extremely threatened by change. My parents' marriage ended in divorce when I was seventeen and consequently I was afraid of anything that appeared to rock the boat. I held on to relationships and unhealthy patterns to ensure a sense of security. In particular I kept up a pattern of pretence to prevent me from having to face change. I would pretend to be happy when I wasn't. I would pretend to feel fine when I was fuming and I would pretend to be honest whilst hiding the truth of my thoughts. If you have done similar things you will know the level of discomfort that it brings.

Rising to the challenge of change means giving up pretence and not hiding the truth. The gift of this is that it makes you authentic in your relationship, which brings freedom and fulfilment. As long as you continue to be inauthentic you will fear change. It is like walking on thin ice and hoping that it won't crack. It does not provide a firm foundation for your relationship because as long as you pretend, you are run by fear.

It takes boldness and courage to stop pretending and to get real in a relationship. Have the agreement to be authentic and honest with each other. This means that when change does arise you have the internal security to handle it. You are both able to reveal your doubts and concerns without overly reacting to them. You are able to be a source of strength and support to each other, which helps the challenge of change. People who rise to the challenge are prepared to give up the status quo and the safe option. I invite you to respond to change in your relationship with courage and boldness. This will enable you to welcome change and rise to its challenge.

Being courageous

Jack had been married for eight years. Before his marriage he had travelled the world with his work and lived a carefree existence. When he came to see me he admitted that although he loved his wife he didn't feel he was in love with her. He confessed that once the honeymoon had passed he questioned his decision, but children arrived and he kept busy with work. He felt restless and unfulfilled, believing that he had made a mistake.

We looked at the changes that he would like to make. Jack's initial reaction was to get a divorce and to move on with his life. I asked him if he had previously experienced similar feelings. He declared that in all his past relationships he had experienced the same feeling and kept moving on to avoid facing the issue. This time he didn't want to brush it under the carpet and he could see that it was an old pattern of his.

I challenged him to be courageous and commit to making a break with the story of his past relationships. He said that the courageous act would be to communicate with his wife, share his feelings of regret and uncertainty, and apologise for running his past pattern in the marriage. His fear was that she wouldn't understand, the relationship would break down and he would lose the children. I asked him to put himself in his wife's shoes and to imagine receiving the communication. He agreed that although she would be hurt and angry, ultimately she would value his courage and it would give them an honest platform to build on.

Jack rehearsed the communication. Initially he felt guilty and afraid so it came out in a blaming and covert way. Having practised it several times he reached a space of authenticity in which he said what he felt, took responsibility for his feelings, apologised for making his wife wrong through wanting to be right about his own perception of the marriage, and committed to creating an honest and loving relationship.

He reported back several days later that he had been courageous and talked with his wife. She was deeply upset, feeling let down and betrayed, but she also recognised his courage in making the communication. She felt touched and moved by his sincerity and was willing to commit to strengthening the honesty and love in the relationship. Jack claimed that the outcome was a real breakthrough, because previously he would either have left, or been convinced that it wouldn't have survived such a level of honesty.

There is no doubt that it is a courageous act to step forward with sincerity and integrity to bring about change in a relationship. I often hear people wanting to make changes for the better but being blocked by fear. One of the most powerful lessons to learn is that fear doesn't disappear, but your courage in feeling the fear and acting anyway creates the climate for change to occur. Fear is part of being human. As you accept the feeling of fear you free yourself from it and empower yourself to be courageous and bold.

It is also a courageous act to be on the receiving end of things that are painful and difficult, and to be big enough to rise above the desire to get angry or vengeful. It would have been understandable if Jack's wife had shown him the door, but her courage enabled them to work their relationship out together.

Consider the difference it would make in your relationship if you were to be bold and courageous. What would you communicate if you felt the fear and acted anyway? How would you express yourself if you followed your courage? It is worthwhile to ask yourself these types of questions each day, because being courageous is not a one-off event. It is a continuous process that builds on itself.

Set your partner free

One of the most common concerns I hear people express about being in a relationship is the fear of feeling trapped, restricted and constrained. We have come to value our freedom to such an extent that it either causes some people to sit on the fence and not enter a relationship, or, if they are in one, to exhibit possessive behaviour, jealousy and control. This is not true freedom because letting your fear run you keeps you boxed in. So a vital component of a successful relationship is the willingness to set your partner free, which involves the ability to focus on trust, surrender and love.

There is nothing wrong in having short relationships or being single, as long as they are conscious choices and not fearful reactions. To respond with fear in a relationship will keep you separate and prevent you from moving forward. The choice to set your partner free means that you are constantly recognising the fact that you are two human beings who choose to be together. You are both free to make new choices at any moment, which keeps the relationship present and alive.

To perceive ourselves as trapped or limited in any form is essentially a state of mind. Stories of people who have had their liberty removed but were able to feel free are powerful reminders of this fact. In those traumatic situations their survival and sanity depended on their ability to transcend the apparent limitation placed on them and to connect with our greatest freedom – the ability to choose our response in any given situation, to choose our own way.

At one relationship workshop a lady stood up outraged at the idea of setting one's partner free. Mary shared how she had been married for twenty years and in that time had done everything for her husband. She made sure that his dinner was on the table at the appointed time each night, the housework was meticulous and his ironing was done. She claimed that her husband was free to do whatever he wanted but that he still treated her badly. When we probed a little deeper Mary began to realise that although she believed that she set him free, there were many strings attached to her behaviour. She was a perfectionist housewife in order to keep him happy, but was afraid that if she slipped up he would get angry and leave. She didn't express her own feelings due to the fear of being a burden, on the basis that he worked hard and the last thing he needed when he got home was a nagging wife. Although these were worthy aims the result was that she kept herself in a box and prevented her husband from relating to the real Mary.

I asked her to imagine truly setting her husband free and to talk about the picture in her mind that this thought created. Mary saw herself being honest and communicating with him in an entirely new way. She was no longer submissive but confident and expressive; she explained her behaviour and committed to no longer acting out of fear. She began to invest time in her own projects and negotiated with him about doing the domestic chores. I then asked her to imagine how he would respond. She saw him smiling and welcoming her communication. Although there was some initial resistance it was due to the fear of change. He appeared delighted that she wanted to focus on her own life more and it seemed to free him too.

The next step was for Mary to put this into practice. She went home that night to discuss the events of the day. The following morning she disclosed that they had spoken and that she had experienced a real breakthrough. Her openness had enabled her husband to share his feelings about their current situation, which were also far from happy. He had felt controlled by her meticulous housekeeping, which had prevented him from being spontaneous. He believed that she derived her sense of self-worth from working on the house, but in fact he would have rather seen her developing her own life, which he felt would give the marriage a greater equality and sense of adventure. You could almost see the lightness return to Mary as she told of her experience. It inspired many people that day to re-evaluate the positions they held in their relationship, to see if they were as flexible as they had first believed.

To set your partner free is a powerful act of trust. It is a reflection of your inner security and your faith in your partnership beyond rules and roles. It requires open and honest communication to establish clear understanding about the choices being made. Notice if you hold on to your partner out of fear, or if you feel constricted by them. If so, talk about it together in order to find out how you both feel. Often, until you identify a dynamic, it drives a relationship unconsciously. Explain that the purpose of setting each other free is to nourish and strengthen the partnership. It develops trust and means that you are fully aware of how the relationship is constantly changing and developing.

Change your mind, change your relationship

How often have you held on to a stubborn point of view only to find it driving a wedge into your relationship? The need to be 'right' causes more angst than probably any other single factor. See how many of the following 'right' issues you relate to:

- You want to be 'right' about the opinion you have of your partner.
- You want to be 'right' about how things should be done.
- You want to be 'right' about what you eat together.
- You want to be 'right' about what clothes you should both wear.
- You want to be 'right' about your career choices.
- You want to be 'right' about the friends you keep.
- You want to be 'right' about which movie to watch.
- You want to be 'right' about where to go on holiday.
- You want to be 'right' about which side of the bed to sleep on.
- You want to be 'right' about the children's behaviour.
- You want to be 'right' about the financial budget.

Now although your opinion is valid, it does not mean that it is the 'right' one. The need to be 'right' is fuelled by pride and can destroy a relationship if continued over time. The extent to which you are willing to change your mind and see things differently is the extent to which you are willing to create and sustain a successful relationship.

The question to ask yourself on a regular basis is: *Would you rather be right, or happy?* Naturally most people would like both, but given the choice, what would you go for? To choose being right limits your options; it places you in a box that is difficult to escape from because once you have announced your position it becomes impossible to change it without being prepared to change your mind. I have certainly discovered that each time I care more about being right than about being happy I sacrifice the experience of joy and love.

I had a friend who was locked in bitter divorce proceedings. It was a painful process that involved having to agree about the children, division of property and finances. In the middle of it he realised that the major bone of contention was who was 'right' about the breakdown of the marriage. Both parties were blaming each other and neither was willing to accept responsibility for the separation. They were projecting the need to be 'right' on to a proceeding that was paying their lawyers well and causing them great pain. Following this awakening he was big enough to change his mind about the relationship. He stopped seeing his ex-wife as the enemy and was able to accept their differences. His ability to let go of needing to be 'right' was enough to break the power struggle they were involved in and help them move towards a harmonious divorce.

To prevent a relationship from reaching the pain of a separation, be willing to change your mind on a daily basis. This means developing the ability to see things from both perspectives, and keeping a fresh outlook. Naturally you are not going to agree with everything your partner says or does; and accepting this fact gives the relationship breathing space and allows it to grow in healthy ways.

If you have ever experienced your relationship as stagnant, changing your mind about it means that you don't necessarily need to change the relationship itself. I have witnessed many people ending a relationship only to start a new one and recreate the same patterns they had just left. This is because until you are prepared to change your mind you will continue to have similar experiences.

I worked with a couple called Paul and Rose who experienced a new level of partnership as a result of their willingness to change their minds about each other. They have their own business and therefore spent most of their time together. Rose is the visionary in the business, generating new ideas and keeping it at the forefront of their profession. She is very sociable, enjoying other people's company which she finds stimulating and fun. Paul is the methodical type, providing stability and an attention to detail. They were getting on each other's nerves and had a long list of complaints about each other. Rose claimed that Paul was too narrow in his outlook which she found restrictive, and Paul said that Rose was unrealistic, providing unnecessary pressure. By working with the principle of changing their mind they were able to see each other differently and to value their uniqueness once again.

The process of changing your mind removes blinkers from your vision. I used to be afraid of a long-term relationship because I believed that it would become stale. The turning point came when I reflected on the relationship that I had with myself, which I hoped would be a permanent fixture. I realised that if I could continue to change my mind about myself for the better then I could apply the same principle to a relationship. It simply takes a large amount of willingness and a small amount of how to change your mind for the better.

8

Remember What's Important

THE PRINCIPLE OF PRIORITIES

I used to love flying as a child. The thrill of being in an aeroplane, looking down upon the world – there was nothing quite like it. Now I find that there is a moment just before landing when I catch myself wondering: 'What if we don't land safely? What if this is the last few minutes of my life?' In that moment I ask myself: 'If I were to die what would I regret?' The overriding answer is not to have made the most of life whilst I had the chance.

I believe that when people reach the end of their life and they look back, they tend not to wish that they had spent an extra hour in the office, or that they had saved an extra amount of money. They reflect upon what is really important: relationships, family, health, happiness, love, peace and making a valuable contribution. However in today's world we are in a rush. We are making haste. We are keeping busy. And we forget what is really important. Our priorities are focused on getting ahead, making more money, achieving more success, accumulating more things. I'm not saying that there is anything wrong in progress, achievement and wealth, but we must watch the price that we pay for them.

In a relationship when we forget what's important, love fades, arguments rule, conflict abounds and hurt ensues. People feel let down, betrayed and disillusioned. Excuses are made such as: 'I'm doing this for us', 'Soon it will be okay', 'Once I've achieved this goal I'll stop'. Yet life isn't so black and white. Unless we make new choices today and refocus our priorities it's only too easy to let what's important slip by.

As you read this chapter let it inspire you to put what's important at the centre of your existence. Don't wait until you reach a crisis to follow your priorities. Seize them.

Living a life of gratitude

Bob and Martha have been married for over twenty years. Their relationship is a role model of what it is possible to create in the realm of relationships. They are deeply in love with each other, affectionate and caring. They bring out the best in each other as parents, grandparents, in their careers and in the community. When I asked what ingredients make their relationship so inspiring, they said that the key is never to let a day go by in which you fail to acknowledge and express your sincere gratitude for having the gift of your partner in your life. Even when they have hit rocky periods, they claim that what carried them through has been their devotion to each other, spearheaded by their gratitude.

We have to watch out because it is easy to forget to be grateful for the gift of our partner. When we hit rush-hour in our lives we can overlook the love, tenderness, support and strength that they bring us. In the back of our minds we tell ourselves that we'll express our gratitude when we have the time. This is backward thinking. Gratitude is a priority that must be recognised as such in order for a relationship to succeed. As soon as we stop being grateful, we disconnect from the appreciation that we have for our partner, and this is when upsets can blow up out of all proportion.

Gratitude is not a quick fix technique that covers up cracks in a relationship. It is a way of being that focuses your attention on appreciating everything that comes your way – even those moments that you didn't bargain for. In one seminar, a couple shared how they had lost everything as a result of a failed business. Their house was repossessed, and their car, and their furniture. They had two young children at the time and their backs were up against the wall. They managed to survive with the help of family and friends, and rebuilt their life. In retrospect they said that they were grateful for what had happened because it had forced them to completely rethink their life and that they now had a balanced, rewarding lifestyle. They spent more time together as a family, they didn't worry about little things when they surfaced and they contributed to their local community in ways they had previously been too busy to consider.

Since it often happens that you only remember what is truly important as a result of a crisis, the onus lies on yourself to choose to be grateful for what you have in your life today. Commit to gratitude and discover a new meaning and joy that only gratitude can bring about. Being grateful enables you to live fully today. It keeps you in present time and focused on what's important, rather than getting caught up in meaningless goals which create meaningless consequences.

One of the exercises at The Happiness Project that has generated the most positive response is keeping a 'gratitude journal'. This is a book in which you note what you are grateful for each day. To do this as a couple gives you a focus and reminds you to make gratitude a priority in your life. There is no order to the importance of things to be grateful for. It can be as simple as walking the dog, the gift of waking up each new day, sharing a life of love together. The key is to make sure that your choices are genuine (and to do it even on days when you're not in the mood).

The gift of happiness

When you are happy you touch gratitude from moment to moment. In fact gratitude is probably one of the fastest tracks to happiness. As co-director of The Happiness Project I have the opportunity to see how important happiness is to relationships, in particular the relationship between being happy with oneself and being happy with our partner. Unless you are happy with yourself you will not be happy with your partner. Although this can sound quite extreme, if you are not happy with yourself you project that unhappiness on to your partner and believe that they are the source of it. This is an erroneous belief, which can cause havoc if it is not recognised and dealt with.

Charles came to see me at a troubled time in his relationship. He had been with his partner for nearly two years and was now deeply unhappy and wanted to leave. When I asked for details he proceeded to tell me how his partner held him back; she was too reliant on him emotionally and too demanding of his time. I asked if he had experienced this before, to which he replied that every previous relationship had ended up in the same boat. Alarm bells sounded in my head. It was time to find out how Charles felt about himself. What transpired was that he didn't feel good enough and therefore whenever a relationship deepened, he left so that he didn't have to experience his self-doubt. Each new relationship gave him the chance to have another honeymoon period, which always left him back in the same place. With this new understanding Charles recognised the importance of being happy with himself in order to break his habit.

The process of being happy with yourself is a process of remembrance. We are happy 100% of the time – however, our awareness of it comes and goes. Unfortunately our society does not encourage us to remember this. We are told that if we accumulate x amount of stuff, achieve y amount of accomplishments and earn z amount of money we'll be happy. Therefore we go off in search of happiness. But the pursuit of happiness will always fail because happiness is not to be found in things; happiness is in you.

I am not saying don't go out and accumulate, achieve and earn – far from it. At least you can arrive at your problems in style. But don't bank your happiness on it. Ultimately happiness is a choice that only you can make. No one or no thing can make you happy. Your partner can encourage you to be happy, doing work you love can remind you to be happy, contributing to the good of society can help you to be happy – but none of these things can make you happy.

I thought that I would be happy when I left music and moved

into the field of psychology. I believed that I would be happy when I bought my first home. I hoped that I would be happy when I first appeared on TV. I prayed that I would be happy when I got married. I was convinced that I would be happy when I became director of The Happiness Project. I was certain that I would be happy when I became a published author. Now all these things have helped, but unless I choose to be happy there will still be something missing.

Imagine the world wide web of happiness. It is always there, always available – but if you don't log on you miss out. This is a paradigm shift from believing that happiness is something that you have to work for, deserve, earn and pay for. These are the most common limiting beliefs about happiness, which block your experience of it. Making this shift opens you to new possibilities for happiness, which go far beyond the rat race and the fast lane.

The most important key to happiness is self-acceptance. Without self-acceptance happiness is impossible because the voice of judgement keeps you from it. We have been trained to be hard on ourselves. We are probably so critical and often so damning of ourselves that if we talked to others the way we talked to ourselves we certainly wouldn't have any friends. Self-acceptance gives yourself a break. It is being aware of the relentless voice in your head telling you that you're not good enough, attractive enough or smart enough. That voice is the perfectionist that lets you know that you don't do a good enough job whatever you achieve, and warns you that if you do accept what you do then you're going to fall behind. Self-acceptance is the application of love, without which it is difficult to receive somebody else's love. Somebody might give you love and you will reject them for being foolish enough to try and love you. It is a syndrome epitomised by Groucho Marx when he declared that he would not join any club that would have him as a member.

A transitional stage towards self-acceptance is forgiveness. When you truly forgive yourself you come to accept yourself for who you are, not who you pretend to be. Forgiveness is to give forth your love to yourself for the purpose of healing your misperceptions of yourself. It is a mistake to see yourself as unworthy of receiving love from a partner, it is a falsity to see yourself as not good enough for anyone else and it is a lie to believe that you are wrong, bad or deserving of punishment in any form. The choice to forgive yourself brings you home to your true self, which is whole and complete.

To forgive and accept yourself are probably the greatest gifts that you can give your partner. It means that you take responsibility for your own happiness and you no longer look toward your partner to make you whole. This breaks through any chains that bind you and allows the relationship to grow in inter-dependent ways.

Forgiveness sets you free

Forgiveness is a shift in perception; it is the willingness to see someone or something differently and to let go of any past grievance or upset. Forgiveness is one of the most challenging principles to apply in relationships because our pride can take over and prevent us from extending it when we feel hurt, angry or betrayed. There are also certain misunderstandings about forgiveness, which prevent us from applying it in our relationships. Forgiveness is not letting someone off the hook, agreeing with abusive or destructive behaviour, or being a martyr. True forgiveness is to look beyond somebody's behaviour and to connect with their innocence and wholeness.

The following example illustrates how we can experience real forgiveness. I had a client who shared the history of how her partner had been unfaithful. Jane said that when she had found out about the affair she had forgiven her partner and taken him back. When I asked her how she felt about the situation she replied that it was fine, but that she was concerned about suffering anxiety attacks and finding it difficult to sleep – a clear indication that in fact things weren't okay.

I asked her about her past. It transpired that her father had had affairs during the marriage and that Jane had watched her mother taking him back each time. She remembered asking her mother about it, who brushed it off with the comment: 'You must forgive and forget.' Jane had internalised this message and had tried to do the right thing in her own mind. It wasn't working because true forgiveness is not just forgiving and forgetting. We often pretend that we have forgotten a grievance when it is buried inside our unconscious.

I asked Jane if she had told her partner how she truly felt. She said that she hadn't because she felt guilty about her thoughts. She saw her partner as a liar and a cheat but she believed that it was wrong to have those thoughts. We did a role-play in which she imagined saying these things to her partner. At first she was embarrassed but slowly began to say how much pain and grief she experienced as a result of the affair, which caused her anxiety attacks and sleepless nights. She expressed her anger and said that she was no longer prepared to tolerate his behaviour.

She accepted responsibility for having pretended to forgive in the past and said that she was now willing to truly forgive and shift her perception of the situation. This was the big step for Jane – to choose to see her partner as he is *now*, and not as he was in the past. When we are angry with people, we are angry because of something they said or did. But what people say or do is not who they are. To let go of a past perception of someone enables us to move forward in our lives, otherwise we relate to them from the past, which keeps both people stuck in it.

The next time I saw Jane she reported back on a conversation that she had had with her partner explaining her position. Although she had been initially afraid of his reaction she found him to be genuinely touched and moved by her communication. He apologised for his behaviour and appreciated her honesty. He thought that he had got away with the affair because she had seemed to forgive and forget. He realised that he had been using her and committed to changing his ways. She explained that she was prepared to let go of the previous judgement that she held about him because it didn't help change the situation. She saw that extending true forgiveness and compassion opens the door to a healed response.

All forgiveness is for you. As you forgive another you set

yourself free. The act of holding on to grievances hurts one person – you. Grievances weigh you down and cause you to want to stay 'right' about your opinion. Being resentful is like taking poison yourself and hoping someone else suffers. It eats away at you and keeps you trapped in the past. Staying angry raises your blood pressure and stress levels. People make mistakes. In a relationship we have to make allowances for being human. Forgiveness is the gift we can give ourselves when we're caught in the darkness.

Remember a time when you truly forgave another person; what happened? What was the response? When I experienced my first major break-up I was devastated. I found it difficult to function personally and professionally and I was furious at my ex-partner, blaming her for the separation. Eventually I realised that the anger was eating away at me and preventing me from moving forward. She was getting on with her life and I was stuck in the past. It was time to apply forgiveness. Firstly I needed to forgive myself for creating the situation. I saw where the relationship had not worked and realised it was a blessing that we were no longer together. Giving compassion to myself helped me to offer compassion to her. I felt myself let go of the anger and resentment that I was carrying and return to my former self. The test came when I bumped into her later and discovered that it was genuinely good to see her and to be able to wish her well.

The following four steps are guidelines to forgiveness in a relationship:

1. Choose to forgive yourself for experiencing the situation in the first place. A relationship is a mirror which reflects back to you your own state of mind, so you have a responsibility for any conflict that you experience. Do not use this information to blame yourself, simply to increase your understanding of the nature of a relationship.
2. Choose to forgive the other person. Since our true identity is not defined by our personality or behaviour, the choice to forgive another is the choice to see who they really are. The starting point is to be willing to see the other person in a

different light. Our interpretation of someone creates our experience of the relationship, so it becomes a self-fulfilling prophecy.

3. Communicate honestly and with compassion. Forgiveness does not mean that you are simply 'nice' and do not express how you truly feel. Being prepared to step forward with your truth builds bridges and repairs broken roads. It also allows the other person to express themselves and to gain greater clarity. Be willing to apologise for your part in the relationship, don't let pride get the better of you.

4. Restore peace to the relationship. If you have forgiven fully, a sense of wholeness and completion is returned to the relationship. Hidden agendas are cleared, damaging communication stops and harmony is restored.

Put friendship first

After my initial brief meeting with Veronica I relied on phone and fax to develop our relationship. What transpired was the opportunity to become firm friends. We spoke with each other as often as we could or wrote long faxes sharing stories about our lives. We got to know each other in a way that might not have been possible had we lived in the same country. My tendency at the time was to become sexually involved early on in a relationship, which intensified it and often prevented the development of friendship. When we finally spent time together there was already a strong foundation that involved wanting the best for each other and celebrating each other's lives. What I value about our relationship today is the level of mutual friendship and support that we share.

Thankfully, you and your partner do not have to live in different countries in order to be great friends. Consciously making friendship a priority ensures that you place each other's interests and well-being at the forefront of the relationship. The function of a true friend is to remind you of what is important when you forget and to appreciate all your qualities, even when you are not putting your best foot forward.

A couple I know deliberately put their worst foot forward at the beginning of their relationship in order to discover if a potential friendship existed. They both had previous marriages with children and there was a lot at stake. They recount how their first few dates together were filled with stories about relationship heartbreaks, their dislikes about various men and women and their hopes and fears. This contrasted greatly with their past when they had simply tried to look good and impress. They discovered that by letting down their defences at a formative stage trust and respect were built as they opened their hearts to each other.

Notice if you try to look good whilst being afraid that if your partner saw all aspects of you they would reject you. Looking good means that you prevent yourself from being authentic, which causes you to feel frustrated and dissatisfied. Taking the risk to be authentic challenges the relationship. A true friend would support you wholeheartedly in taking the risk to reveal all of yourself. A fair-weather friend would want you to compromise yourself if they felt threatened by you in any way.

You can transform the level of friendship within a relationship through your willingness to be honest, forgiving and appreciative. Be honest about how you currently feel about your friendship. Admit to any areas in which you limit yourself and express your commitment to changing those for the better. It's important to explain this in such a way that your partner feels involved and valued. If there is no involvement there will be no commitment from their side. Be willing to let go of unresolved issues in order to allow the friendship to grow. Just because something happened in the past does not mean that it's going to be repeated in the future. Let your partner know what you value about the friendship and what they excel at. People thrive on being reminded about their strengths.

Another way to emphasise your friendship in a relationship is to choose to be celibate for a period of time. Making the conscious choice to abstain from sexual activity gives a relationship breathing space and a chance for the friendship to evolve. I watched this help re-ignite friendship in a couple who had been struggling for some time. In their early thirties, they had two young children and were feeling burdened with responsibility and household chores. They were suffering prickly heat, bickering constantly and blaming each other for the tension. They resisted the idea of celibacy because sex was one of the few areas where they could forget the daily routine. However, they'd reached a stage where they were willing to try anything that might help. They were surprised by the consequences. Initially they agreed to be celibate for 30 days. During that time they found that the pressure seemed to come off the relationship and they started to relate to each other with a new freshness. Energetically it lightened things up and a sense of playfulness resumed. They reconnected with their choice to be together, which had become swallowed up by family life. The benefits were so great that they still continue to choose celibacy when life gets on top of them.

Putting friendship first helps you to prioritise the well-being of your partner and takes the attention away from your own needs. As a friend you want the other person to be happy, which might even mean that you let go of the relationship if they are truly suffering. Occasionally when Veronica and I have reached low points together, a successful strategy has been to remind each other that it is always our choice to be together. We do not have to stay with each other and as real friends who value each other's happiness we are willing to consider this possibility. Coming from this place of unconditional friendship enables us to return to love and this helps us to reconnect with the joy of being together.

Commit to putting friendship first in your relationship. Ask yourself: *'How can I strengthen our friendship?'* Be willing to follow the answer you receive and enjoy the benefits of companionship and love.

Fight/flight or fun!

One of the most important lessons to learn is how to deal with the stress that surfaces as a result of being in a relationship. The traditional response to stress is either to fight it, where we put on our boxing gloves and go the full fifteen rounds, turning up the pressure in an effort to beat it, or to flee from it and hope that it will go away. There is a third option, which is to respond with fun. When stress is present, fun is usually furthest from our thoughts. As Woody Allen once put it: *'Most of the time I have no fun, the rest of the time I have no fun at all.'*

To decide to have fun is the willingness to see stress in a relationship as a personal reminder to make changes for the better. It is an invitation to refocus, re-evaluate and review what's important. So often we put our 'to do' list before fun. We let our lives become dominated by the puritanical work ethic, choosing to wash up, vacuum, pay the bills and do the shopping before enjoying each other's company. I am not advocating giving up anything – simply reminding you to make sure that you are having fun along the way.

I have been addicted to stress in my time. I was driven by the need to clear my 'in tray' before I could have fun in my relationship. Being self-employed and working from home made it difficult to create boundaries which separated me from work. I could keep going all hours and my relationship suffered and stress ensued. I gradually woke up to the fact that even when I die my 'in tray' will have things in it. The art is to organise my priorities so that everything gets done and I have fun in the process.

Some close friends have been good role models for me in this area. The husband works in the pop music industry, which notoriously involves working all hours, living on the road and putting intolerable pressure on relationships. His wife is a clinical psychologist and has extremely clear boundaries in relation to time and priorities. The only way their relationship was going to work was for him to set parameters, which other people would need to respect. At first he experienced con- siderable resistance from colleagues to a nine-to-six routine. However, over time he has become respected for his working hours and it works well. He is able to balance work with having fun in the marriage, which goes to show that it is possible.

I am aware that it is a very real challenge to prioritise fun in relationships. I worked with a lady in her mid-twenties who was so driven in her route up the corporate ladder that she sacrificed relationships altogether. Whenever Caroline did get involved with a man the feed-back she received was that she was too aggressive and dominant. She found that she was carrying her work behaviour into her relationships and it didn't work. I asked her to remember herself as a child. Caroline pictured herself as a playful, carefree girl who loved nothing more than to have fun with friends. We used this image as a reminder that although she had developed a tough exterior, behind it lay a childlike innocence. When she drew upon it she attracted men like flies.

Fun is so important in a relationship that when there is an absence of it, mountains are made out of molehills, communication breaks down and love is hidden behind dark clouds. One of the most popular exercises that I suggest to couples who are locked into power struggles is to schedule in a *fun day*. This is a day devoted to having fun in whatever form that takes. Some couples take themselves off to the seaside, others to the country for long walks and pub lunches whilst others go to art galleries, movies or concerts. The purpose of a fun day is to break the pattern of getting stressed out, which causes you to forget priorities and lose perspective.

One of the most common tendencies when you are stressed is to forget about the very things that support you the most. A wise thing to do is to discover the sources of strength that support you and your relationship and commit to doing them when you experience stress. Sources of strength in life can include hobbies, time for stillness and silence, prayer, reading, sport, eating healthily, rest, time alone, seeing close friends and family. Ensuring that you make your source of strength a priority keeps you on track in your life and relationship.

Think about the sources of strength in your life. What nourishes, supports and invigorates you? Do you make them a priority or put them last on the list when you are stressed? Your commitment to reprioritising what's important to you enables you to be the fun, loving person you are and to bring the best to your relationship.

Keeping things simple

Keep things simple. This is a powerful reminder to return to what's important whenever you catch yourself making life complicated. Keeping things simple means being willing to let go of 'efforting' – or trying too hard. 'Efforting' blocks you from letting good things happen to you in a relationship. It is often caused by a belief in unworthiness – a feeling that you do not deserve to experience the love and joy that you desire. In fact 'efforting' creates the opposite result to the one that you want. For example, if you want to experience intimacy, trying too hard to create it drives people away. Once you let go of the effort the intimacy flows of its own accord. The main cause of 'efforting' is fear. Being stuck in fear makes you try to control the outcomes in your relationship. This usually backfires because others do not respond well to being controlled. It puts unhealthy constraints on your relationship and is a reflection of a lack of trust and feeling of safety.

Your willingness to keep things simple is a reflection of your commitment to remembering what's important. It connects you to the core values that underpin your relationship. A powerful process that you can do with your partner is to decide which values are most important to you, and then place them at the centre of your relationship. Veronica and I did this as part of our preparation before our wedding. We went away for a weekend to give us the space to reflect together. We booked into a romantic restaurant for dinner and took along a notepad to jot down our thoughts. Unfortunately we forgot to keep it simple and found ourselves efforting to get down our values. We got into a power struggle in relation to whose values were more important, which was not a wise move. It spoilt the dinner but ensured that having been through that experience once we were able to clarify them the next day with relative ease and a sense of humour. They became the vows that we exchanged at our wedding and which I would like to share with you now:

We dedicate our relationship to love, truth and simplicity. As

friends and partners we will honour and cherish each other,
holding the space for us to be all that we are. We offer each other
the gifts of playfulness, love and laughter in the sharing of our
lives together. May our relationship be an expression of peace in
the world.

Remembering to follow these vows reminds us of what's important to us. It also means that we are able to keep things simple because we know what we are committed to. Take time with your partner either to review your values or consciously to discover them. Retain your sense of humour and a flexible outlook whilst doing it. It's not a power game to see who is 'right' but a sharing of deepest desires. Writing them in the form of vows adds a further dimension to their influence. You can always change or add to them but it means that you take a stand, which reinforces your intention.

Another great benefit of naming your values is that it makes you *internally driven* rather than *externally influenced*. As we are constantly bombarded with different messages from outside influences it becomes more of a challenge to stay true to what is important to us. Unless you decide what you put at the centre of your world, somebody else will be happy to do it for you.

Brian and Claudia are a great example of a couple who are internally driven. They had been together for six years before they went through the process of consciously discovering their values. They described their relationship as fulfilled but lacking the sense of partnership they wanted in order to take the next step of having children. Upon reflection they agreed that freedom, fun and unconditional love were values they had already internalised. They chose security, risk and playfulness as values to embrace in order to move forward with their quest. They made new choices, clarifying their positions at work and reminding each other that security comes from within. They spoke with other parents about their experience of having children and learnt from the wisdom shared. Finally they decided to take the risk because the only way they were really going to have children was to move into the unknown and to do it. Brian and Claudia now have two beautiful children, which they say they might never have had unless they had agreed to live life from their values.

Keeping things simple is a choice to appreciate each other, life and all its challenges with an open heart and a willing mind. There's no question that if you make this choice as often as possible, both you as an individual and your relationship will benefit greatly.

9

Choose Love!

THE PRINCIPLE OF LOVE

Have you ever found yourself wanting to be more loved? This is not surprising because to be in a loving relationship is a fundamental need. However, it's important to be clear about what we mean by love, because we have been seduced by a romantic version, a blinding love that sweeps us off our feet. This can and does occur, but only in moments. It is not a permanent state and it is different from true love when we are recognised and accepted unconditionally for who we are.

To base a relationship purely on romantic love is a recipe for disaster and probably is at the heart of many a broken relationship. If we do not experience the heightened emotion of romantic love it can cause us to believe that something is missing, which leads to distress, anxiety and broken dreams. It is an illusion to believe that love can disappear. True love is always here; it is your awareness of its presence that comes and goes. The fears, troubles and conflict that we experience in a relationship may cloud this love, but this does not mean that it has vanished.

The combination of committing to resolving difficulties and dedicating your relationship to true love puts it back on track. This requires you to give up any illusions you have about love and to embrace qualities such as respect, kindness, generosity, compassion and forgiveness. Putting these qualities first in your relationship ensures that when you do hit rocky patches you have a strong foundation to fall back upon. Ultimately opening to true love is a choice that only you can make, and it is your willingness to choose it that attracts the gifts it has to offer such as peace, happiness and joy. This chapter helps you to remove the obstacles that may prevent you from making love a priority.

Unconditional love

Have you ever experienced love dominated by close encounters of the conditional kind, love that has a long list of agendas, demands, expectations, ifs, buts, maybes, whens, oughts, shoulds and musts attached to it? If so, you know that it's a painful experience. A condition is a rule you have created, placed between yourself and your achievement of a desired outcome. To love conditionally is one of the most detrimental ways to behave in a relationship because it blocks intimacy, trust, spontaneity joy and happiness by closing the door on true partnership. At the root of most conditions are fear and a need to control. The fear is that if something doesn't happen in a certain way then you won't get your needs met and things will get out of control.

The tricky thing with conditional love is that we may not even be aware that we are bringing it into a relationship. However, if you ask your partner what conditions they experience in the relationship you might receive some valuable feedback. When I asked Veronica if there are any conditions that I make she gently informed me that I have had expectations about the housework, I have made demands to do with finances and I have had 'shoulds' about time spent together, to name a few.

What have been your ways of placing conditions on love? At my workshops some of the popular conditions that people have shared are the following:

- I'll love you if you dress in a certain way.
- I would love you but you might leave me.
- You must be successful in order for me to love you.
- Stop worrying and I'll love you.
- If you get on with my friends I'll show you my love.

◆ You must spend a certain amount of time with me for me to love you.
◆ When you stop spending so much money I'll love you.
◆ If you listened to me more I'd love you.

We're able to stand back and laugh at the conditions we place when we see them in the light of day, but when we are in the thick of a relationship it's a lot more difficult. The key is to be aware of the conditions that you are holding, inform your partner of them, commit to catching yourself when you do slip into autopilot and allow your partner to pull you up when they experience conditional love.

There are two main factors that cause us to love conditionally:

1.   *As children we received disapproval and linked it to love. As adults we believe that being disapproved of and/or disapproving of others is an indication of love.*

See if you relate to the following scene:

Susan, aged six, enjoys painting pictures at the kitchen table. Her mother ignores her because she is busy getting dinner ready and doing the household chores. One day Susan accidentally knocks over her paint, which spills on the floor. Her mother stops what she's doing and criticises her for the spillage. The next day Susan does the same thing and once again her mother tells her off. Subconsciously Susan concludes that getting some attention from her mother, even it's in the form of disapproval, is better than no attention, and links it to love.

Confusing disapproval with love results in frustration and upset. To send out the message to your partner that you disapprove of them is undermining and controlling. To put up with receiving disapproval is a sign of low self-esteem. Notice if you are quick to complain about your partner, quicker than you are to praise. This is a sure indicator that it's time to change your ways and to let go of disapproval.

2. *The belief that there is not enough love to go around.*

This misperception about love is fuelled by a scarcity mentality and is probably the greatest cause of conditional love. It generates the fear that you have to ration the love that you do feel because it will run out and somebody will get hurt. Once again it has its roots in our past conditioning about love which influences us to believe that there is only so much love to go around.

Being aware of the ways that you love conditionally liberates you now to love with no strings attached. This is true love. It enables you to soar to new heights and experience the miracle of loving fully and freely. The experience of unconditional love goes beyond the five physical senses. It takes you into the realm of the heart, which knows no limits or boundaries. The heart is symbolic of life itself; a never-ending beat which has a life of its own. A healthy heart does not require instructions to beat, just as true love does not need a manual to radiate. The willingness to remove the conditions that you have placed between yourself and love is sufficient to open yourself to the joy of unconditional love. Decide today to love unconditionally and let yourself reap the benefits.

Understanding love

Love is not rational. It is supremely irrational and is a force that goes beyond cognition and reason. The power of love inspires you to follow your dreams, to act with courage, to be forgiving and to give generously. In order for you fully to understand love it is important to clear your conditioning about it. You have received different messages about love from a variety of sources including your mother/mothering influence, father/fathering influence, family and society. Being aware of these messages enables you to choose love today which is free from your past conditioning.

I worked with a client called Julie who came to see me in a state of confusion about love. She had recently entered a new relationship that felt right to her in every way, except that she was finding it difficult to handle the amount of love she was experiencing. She wanted to get her running shoes on but an inner voice was telling her to stay. We started off by working on unravelling her conditioning, with a particular focus on any limiting factors she had received. I asked her to complete the following statements:

What my mother/mothering influence taught me about love was . . . Her responses included:

◆ Love hurts.
◆ Love is controlling and manipulative.
◆ You cannot trust love.
◆ Love is the source of pain.
◆ I have to deserve love.
◆ Watch out for the price you pay.

What my father/fathering influence taught me about love was:

◆ Love is all-consuming.
◆ You can have sex without love.
◆ Love distracts you from work.
◆ Love is expensive.
◆ Love is hard work.
◆ Don't expect it to be easy.

What my family influences taught me about love was:

◆ There is not enough love to go around.
◆ If you are manipulative you get the love you want.
◆ Love dies in a relationship.

What society taught me about love was:

◆ You have to earn it by working hard.
◆ You have to deserve it by being a good citizen.
◆ Watch out because you'll pay for it.

As you can see, Julie had received many limiting messages about love. I encouraged her to recognise that none of these were carved in stone and that she could make new choices for herself. As a result of this process she was able to understand that in her current relationship she was responding to love in ways that were influenced by her past conditioning. This was colouring her reality to such a degree that it caused her to want to leave. I suggested that she leave her old love patterns behind before making decisions about the relationship. It was now up to Julie to make her own choices about love, choices that supported and enhanced her life.

Upon consideration Julie's new blueprint for love was:

- Love heals.
- Love is innocent.
- Love sets you free.
- It's safe to trust love.
- There is an abundance of love to go around.
- Love begets love.
- My innate worth is deserving of receiving love.
- Love is a beautiful gift.
- True love is unconditional.

Developing this understanding of love transformed her outlook towards her relationship. She no longer felt that she needed to leave. She could see that it was a wonderful gift that she could grow and learn from. The love that she shared with her partner was in fact the love that she'd always wanted.

Take some time to reflect upon your past conditioning about love. You can use the questions above and add any other major influencing forces from your past, for example religion, education, peers. Doing this enables you to see love objectively and prevents you from letting limiting conditioning block your experience of it.

I experienced a deeper understanding about love as a result of my parents' separation. I had grown up without questioning love. I had taken it for granted within the family. The day that I found out my parents' marriage was effectively over was hugely significant. I felt my world fall apart. I couldn't understand it. The pain was so great. We went through a testing time as we began the journey of recreating our lives. Love became confused. I didn't know if I was coming or going. I felt that I had nothing to hold on to as a reference. Love no longer made sense. I needed to know what was real in the world, what was the truth about love.

My search took me to Israel and to work as a volunteer on a kibbutz in the middle of the Negev desert, where I spent many hours reflecting on the meaning of love and life whilst picking oranges and lemons. On one of our few days off I headed down to Massada, the hill overlooking the Dead Sea. I climbed up while it was still dark in order to watch the sunrise. I sat back on a large stone perfectly positioned to see the sun creep up over the sea. I was still filled with unanswered questions about life and love. I wanted to understand why love could be so cruel and painful and why relationships could be so devastating. In that moment of watching the power of nature reveal itself I asked the question what is real in life, what is true? What came back to me, as if reflected from the sun itself, was *love is real*. My understanding about what's real is that which is eternal, everlasting and untouched by worldly changes. To understand that love is real explains why as human beings we may experience tremendous pain and suffering, and yet continue our faith in love. Pain may run deep, but love runs even deeper.

I realised that even though my family was no longer together, the love remained. Although there was healing and recovery work to be done, love was present. The motivation to resolve the family issues was driven by love. The willingness to confront each other was brought about by love. Now, many years down the line, what remains in the family is love.

Love heals past wounds and grievances if we let it. Love cleanses feelings of guilt, fear and anger if we let it. Love always answers our prayers if we let it. Understanding love is a journey of returning to what is omnipresent, whole and complete. Since love is always available to us, our job is to make ourselves fully available to it.

Letting love guide you

Love has an innate intelligence. It has its own wisdom that you can learn from. Drawing upon the resource of love moves you away from trying to get it, to deserve it, or to possess it and towards letting love guide you in your relationship and life. This means surrendering to its presence and following the wisdom that it offers.

Sometimes it can appear that love is lacking from our lives. When this happens it is important to recognise that it has not disappeared, it is simply that our awareness of the presence of love has temporarily been lost. The process of reconnecting with love is a journey of remembrance. There is no shortage of love in our lives, only a lack of willingness to receive it.

I have some close friends who have applied the principle of letting love guide their relationship. They are both strong-willed independent personalities who found it difficult to navigate the turbulent waters of being together. There was a pattern of letting past conditioning dominate their choices, which resulted in periods of separation and feelings of isolation. Whenever they tried to rationalise their situation it ended in a battle of egos, each trying to prove the other wrong.

Finally they were willing to accept that there must be a better way. They agreed to take periods of silence together rather than attempting rational discussion. At these times they imagined their hearts opening to one another whilst letting the love surface. They listened closely to what came into their minds at these moments. The predominant thoughts consisted of suggestions such as 'relax', 'all is well', 'be patient', 'learn to hear each other without judgement' and 'practise forgiveness'. By following these messages they experienced greater peace and certainty within their relationship. They explained that it was comparable to having a third party witnessing their relationship and bringing to it the objectivity and clarity that they required.

Letting love guide you opens you to the possibility of love inspiring you and supporting you in your relationship. It is like having a team of cheerleaders encouraging you when things don't work out, and celebrating with you when they do. It provides a strong foundation to fall back upon, bringing a sense of inner security and direction to your relationship. There are no guarantees in a relationship today. Marriage has taken a battering, affairs are widespread and unhappiness within relationships is more common than we think.

Relationship problems are not specific to you – they are universal. It is the choices that you make in response to them that makes a difference. For example, choosing to respond with love creates opportunity, whereas choosing to respond with fear creates conflict. The following are three common relationship problems to which I have applied the principle of letting love lead the way forward:

1. *The inability to sustain a successful, loving relationship*

This stems from a sense of unworthiness and it underlies the majority of relationship problems. It is fuelled by beliefs such as 'I'm not good enough', 'I'm not loveable', 'There's something wrong with me', 'I'm a failure', 'I'm wrong', 'I'm guilty' and 'I'm nothing'. These are subconscious decisions that we have made about ourselves as a result of past experience. The outcome is that we create an entire story based on these erroneous beliefs, which cause us to either struggle to attract a relationship or sabotage the relationship that we're in.

To let love guide you here means that you give up your story. You recognise that these are simply beliefs, decisions that you have made and that you can choose to change your mind about yourself. You return to your whole self, an uncarved block with its true potential waiting to be revealed. You learn to smile whenever you notice yourself acting out your story. You ask for help from friends supporting you in going beyond it and you surrender to the presence of love that is always available to you.

2. *The fear of love*

It is ironic that what we desire the most is also something that we fear. We fear that love will be all consuming, that we will lose our identity, that the experience of it will be too much, that love will cause us to lose control of our lives. We forget that this is not real love – it is the fear of love, and as fear only sees itself in everything, it projects itself on to love.

To fear love in a relationship means that you play a push/pull game with your partner. The message that you send out is, 'I want you, but don't come too close because I can't handle it.' You fear intimacy and you fear rejection. It is a lose/lose situation, which presents no solutions. It is a hurtful and frustrating experience that usually results in the breakdown of a relationship because separation appears the only option.

Applying the guidance of love to this problem means that you stop identifying with fear. You recognise that as long as you perceive love through the eyes of fear, all that you will see is fear. Relating to F.E.A.R as *fantasy experience appearing real* enables you to free and release yourself from its grip. The fantasy experience is that love is going to cause pain. It appears real because you have associated pain with love from past heartbreaks. You need to make the distinction that it's not love that causes pain; it's the decisions that you made as a result of past wounds that are the source of pain.

Letting love guide you opens you to the possibility that love is your closest ally in a relationship. Rather than something to be afraid of, it is a source of strength to nurture and cherish. Love brings you everything that you truly want. It inspires companionship, laughter, compassion, abundance and fun. Healing your fear of love enables you to be fully self-expressed, passionate and intimate, and this lets your soul fly free and your heart sing beautifully.

3. *The unspoken rules*

These are the needs, expectations and demands that can crucify a relationship. We have touched on them before but a gentle reminder here is no bad thing. As long as we allow our relationship to be governed by rules it is limited to the conditions that we set. A relationship that starts out with a lot of love and respect can end in chronic pain as a result of this problem.

Letting love guide you means that you make love more important than rules. Although you acknowledge that you do have needs, expectations and demands, your absolute commitment is to let go of control so that it doesn't destroy your relationship. In order to let go of control, make being happy a greater priority than being righteous.

There is nothing magical about letting love guide your relationship. As you practise it over and over again it becomes a natural response. Turning to love connects you to the strength, wisdom and courage that help you to steer your relationship through whichever conditions you face.

Committing to love

One of the greatest fears expressed about relationships is the fear of commitment. We have associated it with entrapment, responsibility or being given a life sentence. It can cause such alarm that some people never commit and therefore miss out on the joy of true partnership.

I was in that category before getting married. I was happily single, enjoyed the dating scene and did not want to get tied down. It all changed when I met Veronica. Suddenly I was in love to such a degree that my bachelor status looked threatened. It was disconcerting because I had to take a look at this thing called commitment. It hit me when we were on holiday for the first time in India. We had gone together with a group of friends. A turning point for me came whilst we were staying in a beautiful town called Pushka next to a sacred lake. I was having a conversation with a friend and expressing my fears of commitment. He had been married for several years and passed on a piece of advice which radically shifted my thinking. He suggested that instead of committing to the relationship, I commit to the principle of love. Making love more important than the relationship means putting each other's well-being first, even to the extent of ending the relationship if need be.

I took this idea on board for myself. I realised that my past fears of commitment had been connected with the form of a relationship or what it looked like externally. Marriage symbolised work and financial responsibility, possible children, having a larger mortgage and family ties. Bachelorhood represented parties, flexible working hours and no ties. Embracing the principle of committing to love connected me to the essence of a relationship – the internal qualities such as companionship, trust, happiness and compassion. Therefore my commitment to putting the internal qualities first meant that whatever form the relationship took, the essence was more important. This was freedom to me, because I could focus on how I wanted it to be.

Probably one of the greatest dilemmas that we face in a relationship is to know if it is right or not. Wondering how long to continue in a relationship that struggles and goes from one breakdown to the next is an exhausting and stressful business. To commit to love gives you a parameter by which to measure if it's worth staying with the relationship or not. If you deeply commit the relationship to love and it continues to be a painful experience filled with doubt and anguish, let go of the form of it. This releases you from feeling that you have to be together to meet expectations, or to look good. I firmly believe that a relationship has a destiny, which will be fulfilled whatever form it takes. The choice to commit to love accelerates its destiny, which means that if it is right for you to be together you will be, and if it isn't you can let go faster.

A further benefit of committing to love lies in the realm of communication. There is no doubt that it is challenging to communicate with empathy on a consistent basis. Your willingness to commit each communication to love ensures that whatever the outcome love prevails. I observed this in action while working with a couple who were contemplating marriage. They were facing a variety of issues which were preventing them from setting a date. The breakthrough came about when they chose to commit to love and let go of their attachment to form. Their communication was transformed as they stopped trying to justify their positions and opened their hearts to each other. They began to listen in a new way. No longer coloured by their past concepts they described it as if they were hearing each other for the first time. Their relationship was reborn in a spirit of love and trust, enabling them to end the procrastination and to move ahead with grace.

Your willingness to commit to love is an expression of a genuine desire to experience a new freedom and excitement in a relationship. It is comparable to freewheeling down a hill with absolutely nothing to lose and everything to gain. Make sure that you discuss it with your partner in order to have a clear understanding about the principle, then let the wisdom of love guide you in having a loving and successful relationship.

The gift of love

The greatest treasure that you can offer anyone is the gift of love. It enriches, inspires and moves us in ways that only love can. In my marriage we tell each other 'I love you' countless times during a day. At first I feared that it would lose its meaning, or that it was a sign of insecurity – especially because it's not a particularly British thing to do. What I have discovered is that expressing it strengthens our connection to love and constantly reminds us of our dedication to it.

In a world where there is so much pain, suffering and hardship giving the gift of love is extremely precious. Many people have inspired me with their capacity to influence the world with love. Mother Teresa said: *'For this purpose we have been created: to love and to be loved.'* Martin Luther King put it this way: *'Everybody can be great . . . You only need a heart full of grace. A soul generated by love.'* And Mahatma Gandhi expressed it in a statement on non-violence. He said: *'The very first step in non-violence is that we cultivate in our daily life, as between ourselves, truthfulness, humility, tolerance and loving kindness.'* You do not need to be a world leader to spread love, but you do become a leader in your world when you dedicate your life to love.

Reflect for a moment on all the gifts of love that you receive –

friendship, compliments, support, encouragement, hope, fun and a listening ear. If for any reason you feel that you are not receiving such gifts, it's a sure sign that you have either stopped giving them to others or that you need to become a better receiver. There are no special prizes for being a martyr in this life. Letting yourself receive means that you have more to give and letting yourself give means that you have more to receive.

Love works. When you stop giving and receiving gifts of love you may notice that life turns pear-shaped. Your priorities slip, you become hurried, hostile and humourless, and ultimately your life can reach a crisis of meaninglessness. If you reach this stage, you can be sure that you have forgotten to put love first. Reconnecting to the gift of love brings you back to what is truly important. There is no genuine friendship in a relationship without love, no true peace without love, no real joy without love, no heartfelt intimacy without love. Are you aware of this? Are you willing to prioritise love in your life?

It is also helpful to remember that some gifts come badly wrapped. When we have suffered a heartbreak, loss, a painful argument or a separation we do not appreciate the suggestion that there may be a gift involved, however, once the pain has lessened we are in a position to look at it differently. The heartbreak might be an opportunity for greater honesty and integrity; the loss may be making way for something better; the painful argument could be an opening for real understanding; the separation may be freedom in disguise. Your ability to recognise the gifts of love ensures that your life flows like water through rivers, over rocks and into vast oceans.

In my Relationship Intelligence seminar there is a powerful exercise connected to the gifts that we bring to each other in all our relationships. It is a meditation that enables you to gain clarity about the gifts that you are here to give and the gifts that you are to receive. The following is a written version which helps you to be aware of these, to make peace where there was conflict in a relationship and to celebrate joy where there is already harmony:

Sitting in a comfortable position, close your eyes and focus on your breathing. Allowing it to become open, full and free, feel your mind and body relaxing. Picture in your mind's eye your father/fathering influence. See him in front of you. Look deeply into his eyes. Notice what you see and how you feel. You are about to have a conversation with him. It could be one of the most meaningful conversations you have had with him. Set the intention for the conversation. In this moment dedicate it to love, let love be more important than what's happened in the past. Be willing to reach out to your father and let him in. Opening your heart, say to your father: the gifts that I have received from you are . . . Picture yourself telling him the gifts that you have received, maybe it has been the gift of strength, security, protection, vision, inspiration or integrity. Now be aware of the gifts that you have brought to him: your love, friendship, achievements, wisdom. See yourself sharing these gifts and then let the image of your father fade.

Now bring the image of your mother/mothering influence into your mind. Picture her in front of you, looking into your eyes. What are the gifts that she has given to you? Imagine saying to her: the gifts that I have received from you are . . . Take this opportunity to inform her. Perhaps it has been her unconditional love, nurturing, compassion, fairness and courage. Now let yourself acknowledge the gifts that you have given her: your joy, companionship, success, love. Picture the exchange of these gifts and let that image go.

Now see your brothers and sisters in your mind's eye. What are the gifts that they have touched you with? Imagine yourself receiving them. What are the gifts that you have brought them? Picture them receiving your gifts with an open heart.

Next bring your partner or most recent partner into your consciousness. Hold them in front of you. What are the gifts that they have shared with you? In this moment let yourself fully receive them – their love, support, sexuality, playfulness, trust and vision. Now see them receiving your gifts of tenderness, companionship, appreciation and happiness. Breathe deeply.

Move on now to your friends and colleagues. See who comes into your mind. What are the gifts that you have given them and received? Take a moment to listen and notice what moves you.

Finally the children in your life, either your own children or children you know. What are the gifts they have offered you and what have they received from you? See yourself fully receiving their gifts of innocence, love, joy and playfulness and giving gifts of guidance, security and trust.

You are a gift bearer. Commit to giving and receiving the gifts in all your relationships fully.

When you are ready, take several deep breaths, slowly open your eyes and stretch your body.

Being available to the gifts that you have to offer and to receive is what love is all about. Love heals, love inspires, love supports, love moves mountains. Letting your relationship be guided by the power of love lies at the heart of a successful relationship.

10

The Spirit Zone

THE PRINCIPLE OF SPIRITUALITY

One of the major issues on people's minds today is that of meaning. Questions such as 'why are we here?' and 'what is the purpose of life and relationship?' tug at our consciousness as we search to find a meaning greater than that implied by the conveyor belt of life. Many people have achieved an unprecedented level of material wealth and accomplishment of goals, yet still feel that something is missing. What fills this void is a spiritual fulfilment, which goes far beyond the rat-race. (The trouble with the rat-race is that even if you win you still end up a rat.)

My search for meaning has been the driving force behind my work and relationships. When I entered the world of psychology and personal development I wanted to be 'enlightened'. I wanted answers to the multitude of problems that I experienced and witnessed around me. Along the way I have learnt that 'enlightenment' is not a sudden flash of lightning, but a gradual process of lightening up and not taking things quite so seriously. It also doesn't mean that you have to go and live in a cave in the Himalayan mountains, but rather to learn to integrate your vision and your values into your daily life.

To apply the principle of spirituality in a relationship is a commitment to sharing the path to qualities such as love, compassion, trust and joy. By developing the awareness that your relationship has a deeper meaning than meets the eye, and that an important aspect of being together is to discover what that meaning is, expands your partnership.

Although spirituality may be expressed through formal

religion it has no necessary connection to it. Whatever your religious preference, placing spirituality at the centre of a relationship will only enhance your experience of it. This chapter focuses on resolving the crisis in meaning that we often feel, and aims to help build the foundation for a spiritually intelligent relationship that can respond to an age of uncertainty with confidence and serenity.

Learning to let go

Learning to let go is at the heart of spirituality. The idea of letting go usually conjures up an image of defeat. It is often associated with making compromises, being a martyr and inhibiting freedom. This is the opposite of truly letting go, which consists of being willing to soften your own viewpoint, being open to other ways of looking at things and being flexible in your approach. It also requires you to give up old habits that don't support you and to create new possibilities for what you really want.

John was a client who resisted the idea of letting go. He claimed that previously whenever he had let go in his marriage he was taken to the cleaners. I asked what letting go meant to him. He replied that it involved giving up his freedom, backing down in conflicts and apologising incessantly. When I suggested that there could be another way of looking at it, he could understand it intellectually but still rejected the idea. Being stubborn and holding on were survival positions for John. His past experience locked him into a mode of being that kept him safe but unfulfilled.

I suggested that he create a new picture in his mind of letting go. I asked him to visualise it, and become aware of what it genuinely feels like to let go. He was surprised at the outcome. He saw himself communicating with his wife without his traditional defensive response. As a consequence she was loving and open. I asked him to repeat this visualisation until he felt sure that he could bring it into his marriage. Back in the relationship he started consciously to let go when old triggers arose, such as needing to make decisions and resolve disagreements. He was able to release his previous stubborn position and was pleasantly surprised to find that nothing detrimental happened, in fact it brought him closer to his wife.

Common distinguishing features of a stubborn attitude include mentally saying things like:

- I can't stand this any more.
- You are deliberately trying to hurt me.
- I know better than you so why not just follow me.
- You don't understand me.

Emotional traits include:

- Symptoms of stress such as irritability, anxiety, exhaustion, short temperedness, physical tension and burn-out.
- Feelings of anger, fear, doubt and frustration.

The following are behavioural traits common to holding on:

- Walking out of rooms and slamming doors.
- Shutting yourself away in the name of work or a hobby.
- Watching endless television.
- Not scheduling quality time together.

Raising your awareness that you are holding on to a stubborn position accelerates the process of letting go. Perceiving these traits as powerful reminders to let go turns them from potential upsets to opportunities for spiritual development. Instead of telling yourself the same old stories, you can use the following formulae to move forward:

- Mentally I soften my position in order to increase tolerance and patience.
- I perceive you as my teacher, friend and lover, which may mean that you say things that I resist initially, but which are for our highest good.

- I am open to new learning and insights that are mutually beneficial to us.
- Our understanding grows as we let go and focus on love.

On an emotional level ask yourself:

- What are my emotions telling me?
- How I can learn from them?
- How are they serving me?

If an emotion is overwhelming say to yourself:

- I am with the feeling of —, while understanding that I am not my feelings.
- Even this feeling will pass.
- Take deep, measured breaths, letting the breath relax as you exhale.

On a behavioural level make the following changes:

- Stop actions fuelled by anger that may cause future harm or regret.
- Stay open all hours for the good of the relationship.
- Turn the television off when it becomes a distraction. Instead cook together, spend time in nature, appreciate art and music.
- Schedule quality time together, ensuring that you have quiet time on a regular basis.

As you implement these ideas you will naturally find yourself surrendering, trusting and experiencing greater honesty, which brings a new dimension of love to the relationship. Your passion is rekindled as energy is freed and released. You are able to lighten up and laugh at everyday events. Remember that it is your intention to let go that sets this in motion and it is your willingness that carries it forward.

Being compassionate

Linda is an extraordinary example of compassion. Spending time with her makes you feel good. Wherever she goes, whatever she is doing and whoever she is with, she exhibits loving-kindness. It is a remarkable feat because discovering the obstacles that she had to overcome is a humbling experience. She grew up in a violent neighbourhood in a family that offered no protection. Her father was an alcoholic who was physically and sexually abusive to her and her siblings. He was promiscuous in his marriage and her mother suffered in silence, as it would have been sacrilege to give the family a bad name. Linda married a man similar to her father. On the surface he appeared gentle and caring, however behind closed doors he was angry and violent, beating her and undermining her every move.

Finally it reached the point where Linda feared for her life. She had to make a move. She sought out professional help which gave her the courage to leave. Soon afterwards she found out that she had cancer. Her ex-husband's response was to blame her for the illness and to inform her that it was an inconvenience to his life. He even used the cancer against her in the divorce settlement, trying to alter the financial arrangement. Linda was on her knees. She was on the verge of giving up when she attended a cancer support group that opened her to ideas including letting go of guilt, using forgiveness and developing compassion. These are healing resources when you are faced with the trauma of cancer. They give you the gift of hope when you're surrounded by darkness. She discovered that by choosing to forgive her father, her ex-husband and her past experiences she started to reclaim a sense of power. Over a period of time she no longer saw herself as a victim but as a beacon of hope for others.

When I met her at a cancer conference I asked her what was the wisest thing that she had learnt about being compassionate. She paused for a moment, smiled gently and replied, '*Loving as if there is no tomorrow, giving up all need for righteousness, treating others as you would like to be treated, seeing yourself as a part of a whole.'* I remind myself of her wisdom when I catch myself wanting to close down, be 'right' or stay independent. Although living a compassionate life might not sound glamorous, in practice it transforms a relationship. It enables you to develop a rapport that you could only have previously imagined and it brings you an experience of peace which fills your heart and soul.

One of the major resistances to being compassionate is the mistaken belief that it is a form of sacrifice. The distinction between compassion and sacrifice is that compassion is giving from the heart whereas sacrifice is giving out of guilt. When you give from your heart you discover an endless capacity to extend yourself to others, whilst letting go of the limits involved in seeing yourself as an isolated individual. You recognise that you are part of some larger, deeper, richer whole that gives a new perspective to a relationship. This sense of wholeness nourishes you; it feeds your soul and strengthens your connection to others.

To apply compassion is the practice of forgiveness and loving-kindness. As we have discussed, forgiveness is the master eraser, it wipes out the unloving thoughts and actions from the past and reconnects you to the original love. Forgiveness is to give forth your love like a mountain spring releasing fresh water. As your love flows it washes away grievances, leaving you rejuvenated and restored.

Loving-kindness lies at the heart of Buddhist teachings. The following meditation is an ancient practice using repeated phrases, images, and feelings to evoke loving-kindness. It centres on you because once you have connected with loving-kindness then that becomes a natural expression of yourself. To use this meditation it is important to be patient and accepting of yourself, noticing what thoughts or feelings arise in response to this whilst gently bringing your attention back to the practice. The key to the meditation is the intention and attention that you bring to it – you cannot do it wrong.

Sit in an upright, comfortable position. Let your body relax by taking several deep, long breaths. Be aware of any distracting thoughts or feelings, watching them as if they were a movie on a big screen that gradually fades and disappears. Then begin to say inwardly the following phrases. Repeat them over and over for five or ten minutes once a day in a quiet place for several weeks:

> May I be filled with loving-kindness.
> May I be well.
> May I be peaceful and at ease.
> May I be happy.

Once you have focused on yourself for a period of time you can expand the focus of your loving-kindness to your partner. Picture them and say the same phrases:

> May he/she be filled with loving-kindness.
> May he/she be well.
> May he/she be peaceful and at ease.
> May he/she be happy.

This meditation acts as an anchor for you, linking you to love. It is especially useful at times of need, if you are experiencing a conflict, a communication difficulty, or a power struggle. Committing to loving-kindness at these moments reconnects you to what is really important – putting compassion at the heart of your relationship.

Witnessing the journey

When I grew up I believed that I would fall in love and live happily ever after. I was under the illusion that there would be an instant in time, like switching on a light, which would illuminate my life to such a degree that I would never have to worry again. It's a lovely dream but not realistic when you get into the mechanics of sharing your life with someone else. However, if you get too focused on the logistics it can remove you from the love that is present. There is a state that allows you to handle the necessities of daily life without losing the joy of innocent love. It is a state of awareness that enables you to observe your relationship objectively. It is a quality of attention, which places you outside your relationship as well as at the centre of it. This state is known as mindfulness. It is the development of a silent witness within yourself that watches all and judges nothing.

The key to mindfulness is the ability to release attachment to your relationship. In its mildest form attachment is the desire to be with someone special. In its extreme form attachment includes possession, jealousy, control, suspicion and distrust; features which damage and often destroy a relationship. We usually oscillate between these two extremes, however even mild attachment has its limitations as it warps your sense of perspective. In comparing attachment to love, you will see the differences and understand the benefits of creating detachment, or the ability to witness the journey of your relationship.

◆ Love allows you to celebrate the unique differences between you and your partner. Attachment causes you to judge the differences, needing conformity of opinions and behaviours.
◆ Love asks for nothing and embraces everything. Attachment puts conditions, demands and expectations between you and your partner.
◆ Love lets the relationship grow and transform. Attachment keeps you in a familiar comfort zone, perceiving change as a threat.

Focusing on detachment allows you to be aware of three main positions that you can take in a relationship, which give you powerful resources to utilise. The three positions are:

1. The dreamer
Dreaming is the creative dimension of a relationship. Using your imagination enables you to both generate ideas and future possibilities, which can turn into reality if you stay detached about them.

2. The realist

Having a realistic attitude and approach makes things happen. It puts plans into action and makes them real. The position of realist is developed by learning what works from past experience and gaining information from others.

3. The evaluator

The ability to evaluate the success of a plan or idea, think about the pros and cons, and note its strengths and areas where you could do something different helps you to make good decisions about the viability of your ideas. Developing detachment enhances the process of evaluation because it enables you to remain objective and thus to move forward in the right direction.

I have some close friends who are inspiring examples of how to practise detachment and use these resources. Andy is a dreamer. He is a man of vision who conjures up exciting possibilities through his ability to be creative. His wife Susan is a realist. She grounds his ideas and helps to makes them concrete. She loves to plan and follow up by taking action. They have learnt how to step back and evaluate together. They schedule time to look at their ideas and plans objectively, whilst being aware of the pitfalls of becoming overly invested in a particular outcome.

If you are interested in developing the quality of detachment, it is valuable to reflect on which position represents you at your strongest. Then by checking to see where your partner's strengths lie you can support each other. For example if you notice that your partner is stronger as a dreamer, let them play with ideas and possibilities. Encourage them to take the space they need to dream. Becoming conscious of these positions increases your ability to be detached. It is a state of mindfulness that enables you to witness your relationship rather than trying to control it.

Another powerful way to develop mindfulness is the practice of meditation. Since we live in a hurried world, meditation is a helpful way to slow down and witness the journey instead of getting swept away by it. There are a variety of techniques that you can use to meditate, including using the breath or a mantra (a word or statement). The purposes of these tools are to focus your mind, to relax your body and to be in present time.

The practice of meditation involves:

1. Sitting in an upright position, either in a chair or on a cushion, with your eyes closed.
2. Focusing your attention on a specific tool. For example if you choose the breath, simply watch it, noticing its quality as you inhale and exhale. Breathe slowly, taking 6–8 breaths a minute. If you choose a mantra use a word that inspires you, such as peace, love or calm, and repeat it silently in your mind.
3. Letting go of judgement. Notice the inner conversation that takes place in your mind. This is not good or bad, right or wrong, it just is. The most important factor is not to enter the conversation by placing a value judgement on it. To witness it silently removes you from the centre of it.
4. Continuing for up to 20 minutes, once a day, preferably first thing in the morning.

To meditate with your partner adds value to your relationship. It makes you available to the spiritual dimension of life whilst giving you the benefits of relaxation and quality time together. Don't worry if you experience initial resistance. I used to struggle with making the time to meditate. I would conjure every conceivable excuse why it was not possible: I was too tired, I had too many things to do, it was a waste of time. The turning point came for me when a friend who is a teacher of meditation shared an amusing way of approaching it. He calls it 'diarrhoea time'. Obviously when you are suffering from diarrhoea there is no question of whether you have the time to go or not, it is an absolute priority. Give meditation the same importance and making the time will no longer be a dilemma. Couples who share the practice of meditation claim that it helps them to drop defences, to keep their hearts open, to allow any friction they may have between them to dissolve and to strengthen their commitment to their value systems.

Remembering that a relationship is a journey and developing the silent witness means that you can navigate any highs and lows with greater ease and acceptance. There is an old Chinese saying by Lao-Tzu: *The journey of a thousand miles must begin with a single step*. Taking the step to develop detachment is a worthwhile investment for sustaining a successful relationship.

A sense of meaning

See if you relate to the following scenario:

You work hard to pay the mortgage, to create a future for your children and to have a quality life. However, fulfilment seems to elude you. It doesn't seem to matter what you achieve, what you accumulate or where you are, nothing ever seems to be quite enough. This constant pursuit to get ahead in the world is exhausting and relentless.

I have heard this type of dilemma over and over again, maybe expressed in different ways, but all pointing to the same issue – a crisis in meaning. Without a clear sense of meaning, managing daily tasks is demoralising, living with unpredictability is terrifying and having a relationship is stressful. Therefore it is not a luxury but a necessity to have a clear sense of purpose and meaning to steer you forward in life.

The biggest challenge to discovering a meaning is the search involved, which can cause uncertainty and result in taking a road going nowhere. A solution that has brought considerable relief to me is to give up this search and to *choose* a meaning instead. Prior to this understanding, much of my time was spent trying to figure out the supposed meaning of things. If somebody behaved or communicated in a certain way I would analyse the meaning of it. Now I am aware of the meaning that I am choosing to give a behaviour, communication or relationship, and if it isn't useful to the situation I choose to give it another meaning. For example, I used to be quite possessive. If I was in a social situation and my partner at the time was speaking to another man I would interpret it that she was more interested in him than in me. Now I feel completely relaxed when Veronica interacts with other men because I no longer perceive it as a threat. Simply put, the meaning attached to anything, is the meaning that *you* are giving it. This is your greatest freedom. If you experience a crisis in meaning in a relationship you can choose to give it a new meaning that enhances and supports you.

Robert came to see me when he was resolving a very painful separation. He had been with Jill for seven years. It had been the most important relationship of his life and he was devastated that she had left. He was going through the motions of his life but was unable to function effectively. He had resigned himself to the idea that it would take a long time to recover and that in the meantime he had to just make the best of a bad situation. Having listened to Robert's story I asked him what it meant to him that Jill had left. He said that it meant he was a failure as a man and incapable of maintaining a long-term relationship. He obviously wasn't important to her and wondered if he would ever find another woman like her.

As a starting point I asked Robert what he believed he needed in order to move forward. Upon reflection, he said 'time'. I questioned him on the meaning that he had given to time. He replied that it was a great healer, allowing memories to fade and putting things into perspective. I asked how much time he thought that he would need. He wasn't sure but said up to two years, having watched a friend go through a similar separation. I could see that he wasn't thrilled by this prospect and asked him if it would be useful to find a better way forward. He agreed that it would, but was uncertain of the likelihood of finding one. I suggested that rather than wait for time to take its natural course he could choose to give the separation a new meaning. Having checked to see if he believed there was any possibility in reuniting (and realised that there wasn't), I asked him about the lessons that he'd learned so far.

Robert admitted that there had been a multitude of lessons. He had entered the relationship with blinkered vision but had become stronger and wiser. He had developed into a more compassionate and loving person for which he was truly grateful. I asked him about the lessons of separation. He could see that he had become too attached to the relationship and was now having to learn to let go. He was learning to ask for help and not to let his pride get the better of him. The crunch came when I encouraged him to give a new meaning to his belief that he was a failure and unimportant. He was reluctant because his reality didn't include evidence for a new interpretation. The idea that the relationship had been a gift to him and that now the separation was causing him to stretch and grow appealed to him. By giving it a new meaning he was able to make peace with the pain and loss of separation.

Even if you are not in a difficult situation, your interpretation of a relationship is at the centre of the meaning that it has for you. If your partner responds differently from you, what meaning do you give this? Do you perceive it as a threat or a gift? Do you welcome it or resist it? It takes flexibility and willingness to give a new meaning to a challenging event. Often we cannot do this on our own and therefore it's advisable to confide in a trustworthy friend or to get some professional support. As creatures of habit, once a specific meaning has become ingrained it can require a big shift to choose a new one.

Think about a new meaning that you could give to a difficult situation you are experiencing right now. What price do you pay by holding on to the old meaning? What benefits are there to be gained from finding a new one? Having the wisdom and humility to apply it will bring you peace and relief.

Getting inspired

To be inspired is to be 'in spirit'. It connects you with the abundant source of creativity and love that exists in the universe. Consider the possibility of having an inspired relationship. What difference would it make to you and to others? How would it contribute to the greater good of humanity?

I have turned I.N.S.P.I.R.E into an acronym for: Integrity. Now. Service. Passion. Innovation. Respect. Empowerment.

These are the types of values that lie at the heart of making a success of your life. Aligning your relationship with them ensures that you are a mutual source of inspiration for each other, personally, professionally, and in every other way. We shall now take a closer look at each quality involved:

Integrity. The *Oxford English Dictionary* defines integrity as wholeness, soundness, uprightness and honesty. Imagine holding your relationship true to those qualities. So often we are tempted to compromise our integrity in the erroneous belief that we're doing our partner a favour by not being completely honest. I have seen this on numerous occasions in my seminars. For example if someone has got away with having an affair, they believe that it would hurt their partner more to know than not. When I have asked what evidence they are using for this decision, it is usually a whim.

One newly-married lady disclosed that she believed her husband was having an affair with his ex-girlfriend. He worked in the town where she lived and saw her on business. His wife realised that to have integrity meant discussing this situation with him. She was afraid to do so because she didn't want to undermine their trust, but could see that it was not particularly strong anyway. She reported back that when she did talk to him about it he was angry and defensive, but when she explained her commitment to having integrity in the relationship, he softened his position. He agreed that integrity was at the centre of a healthy relationship and was prepared to look at his feelings for his ex-girlfriend. He explained that although he wasn't having an affair, he was still hooked into getting attention from another woman, and agreed to stop seeing her.

To have integrity ensures that you follow your conscience, stand by your word and have consistency in your actions. This means that you build a foundation of trust that others respond to. People turn to you at times of need, respecting your opinion and valuing your example. It allows you to feel good about yourself and your relationship, which deepens your experience of love.

Now. Valuing now is the ability to be fully present, making each moment as precious as a sparkling diamond. A powerful method of discovering the importance of *now* is to imagine that the next 24 hours are your last. What would you do? Where would you go? Who would you communicate with and what would you say? One person I worked with replied that he would charter a plane, invite his nearest and dearest, and fly to a beautiful destination. Another said that she would stay home with her partner and just *be* together. Thankfully this is not a reality we have to contemplate. However by cherishing the moment, your partner and life itself *now*, you receive the most from them.

Service. I love the idea of letting your relationship be a vehicle of service to the world. We often get so caught up in our own needs and wants that we forget how privileged we are, even being fortunate enough to be able to read a book. Although many people do have an aptitude for service they often reserve it for special occasions, such as giving to charity or Christmas. Real service is dedicating your relationship each day to the greater good of mankind. It is taking a moment when together you consciously set your intention and allow the principle of service to inspire your thoughts, emotions and actions.

Tom and Jane are an example of a relationship dedicated to serving humanity. They keep an open house, letting people in the local community know that they are welcome to drop in, either at times of need or for a chat. Their children's friends in particular find it reassuring to be able to visit a home that is filled with non-judgement and compassion. They are involved in a variety of activities ranging from campaigning for the greater good of the community by serving on boards and committees to creating opportunities for artists and musicians by organising exhibitions and concerts. When I asked them what was the main benefit they derived from serving in this style they replied, 'to focus on somebody else's needs, to contribute to the fulfilment of someone's dreams is a gift not to be missed. It is always available to us, however we are usually too busy to make it a priority. The act of giving outside your normal circle of influence broadens your horizons. It adds deeper meaning to your own life, and sharing it together in a relationship strengthens your bond.'

Commit to discovering your own specific form of service, whether it involves community work or simply the decision that your relationship is here to add value to others. You will certainly appreciate receiving the gifts that come to you as a result of making a difference in this way.

Passion. To live with passion is a choice to participate fully in the heart of life. It is the willingness to extend out of your comfort zones and to be a risk taker. Imagine communicating with passion, working with passion, playing with passion and loving with passion – what difference would it make to your relationship? To live with passion does not mean that you have to be a loud, extrovert person. Many people who have been an example of living with passion have done so with a quiet intensity that rubs off on others.

Passion is the quality to call upon if you feel that your relationship has got 'stuck' in a rut. The funny thing with getting into a rut is that you never consciously decide to do it. You tend not to wake up and say 'let's get into a rut today.' It creeps up behind you and then one day you realise that you may have been blocked for some time. If you find yourself in a rut it is often an indication that you have stopped growing and learning together, features which are essential to your development. Getting passionate about life and your relationship again gets you out of a rut. Passion can move mountains. It carries you forward on a wave of excitement and anticipation. It is not based on reason or logic, so instead of analysing the rut, be passionate about your next step together and commit to it with your whole being.

Innovation. Who are the most innovative people you know personally, and in what way? How would you describe the quality of their relationship? How do they communicate and what actions do they take? Would it be useful to you to model yourself on their attitudes and behaviour? One of the most effective ways of developing a quality is to find someone in your own life who inspires you and to learn from him or her. The most innovative person I know is a constant source of inspiration. He places creativity at the centre of his world, allowing himself time to dream, stepping out of the box of routine existence and playing with ideas and concepts. His relationship is fun. Naturally he and his partner have their ups and downs, but whenever they are challenged they rise to it with a sense of possibility that creates opportunities previously unseen.

To be innovative does not mean that you have to be a great inventor or visionary, however you do have the capacity to invent future possibilities for your relationship, based on an inspiring vision. Make time to explore a vision of being together. How would you like your relationship to be? Go back to what's most important to you, your core values, and invent possibilities out of them. For example, if freedom is important to you, create the possibility of being free. If you value communication, create the possibility of being fully self-expressed. Don't let the question of how are you going to do it get in the way. Staying focused on your vision, while being flexible and willing to learn, which gives a great opportunity to your powers of innovation.

Respect. Respect is at the heart of a spiritually intelligent relationship. To honour, cherish and love your partner unconditionally is the greatest gift that you can offer. It keeps a relationship alive, free from complacency and righteousness. It also means that you stay focused on qualities that raise a relationship out of mediocrity and make it magnificent. It is a joy to witness and experience a couple who have integrated respect into their relationship. They carry a sense of peace and wellness into situations, which inspires others to do the same.

Steven has been a mentor in my life. He has an extraordinary capacity to respect other people. It does not matter what job someone may have, what his or her background may be, he relates to everyone out of deep respect. Recently he opened a new business. It had been a challenge of mammoth proportions. People had to work around the clock in order to meet deadlines. His wife and family had to sacrifice immediate needs to support the process. The only way that Steven was able to have everyone pulling in the same direction was because he had built up a large reservoir of trust, born out of the respect that he had given. At the party celebrating the new venture, the overwhelming feeling in the room was that of appreciation for the respect generated by the one person committed to this cause. Put respect at the centre of your relationship and enjoy the fruits of standing for something greater than your individual self.

Empowerment. Having an empowered relationship is a natural result of the six previous qualities. To have integrity, to live in the here and now, to come from a position of service, to be passionate, innovative and respectful are expressions of an empowered partnership. It is the paradigm of interdependence, which recognises that the whole of a relationship is greater than the sum of its parts. The thinking and language in an empowered relationship focuses on *we* rather than *I* or *you*. Characteristic statements include: '*we* are in this together'; '*we* can cooperate, *we* can combine our talents and abilities and create a greater future together.'

To be empowered sets you free. You no longer worry about what other people think about you, but focus on the gifts that you have to give and receive. Embracing the idea that you are a gift bearer moves you away from individual concerns, and places your attention on being part of a constant exchange. It is this flow that makes up the rich tapestry in relationships and ensures that there is never a meaningless moment.

Following wisdom

Every relationship has its own innate wisdom. The answers to difficulties and uncertainties lie within it – the challenge is to listen closely enough to let the wisdom be revealed. At The

Happiness Project a powerful exercise used in workshops is to invite participants to stand up and say, 'I am a wise person'. There is considerable reluctance at first, because people believe that it is arrogant to perceive that they are wise. Yet everyone is indeed wise; we just haven't been educated to realise it. We are taught to think logically rather than to feel and listen to the voice of insight within. Once participants start doing this they enjoy the empowerment that it brings. It is an equally powerful concept to acknowledge that you have a wise relationship. Once again it is an idea that we may not have fully considered, yet there are a variety of benefits to be gained, including:

- Developing trust in the relationship
- Drawing on resources that have been previously overlooked
- Having a strategy for resolving conflict
- Giving a framework for handling doubt and uncertainty
- Creating a state of harmony and peace.

There is nothing that wisdom cannot do. It will guide you to make the right choices at the right time. It helps you detach, to let go and to open yourself to new possibilities. It steers you in the direction of your vision, allowing you to realise the true potential of your relationship.

You are probably thinking this is all very well, but how do you follow wisdom, and when do you know if it's wisdom or wishful thinking? There are three steps to following wisdom:

1. Be prepared to see yourself and your relationship as wise. Your willingness dissolves resistance and opens the door for wisdom to reveal itself.
2. Suspend doubt. Put your uncertainties to one side and listen carefully to the voice of wisdom within.
3. Share your thoughts with your partner. If they resonate with him or her and are met with an affirmative response, follow the wisdom.

Probably the wisest thing that I have learnt about a relationship is that it is a journey. If you join together with your partner in sharing a vision, following similar values, accepting the highs and lows, then you can travel into the future with clarity and confidence.

In Conclusion

There is hope. No matter how challenging a relationship may be, your willingness to start applying these ten principles will put you firmly on the path to relationship success. You don't have to trade in your current partner for another one, you don't even have to wait until you have a relationship; by taking one step at a time, you move forward in the right direction.

There is a wise saying: If you do what you've always done, you'll get what you've always got. Being prepared to do things differently and see the world afresh through a new thought, a changed perception, a touch of willingness, or an act of courage can transform your relationship experience forever.

Further Information

Ben Renshaw is an inspirational speaker, seminar leader, success coach and broadcaster. He travels the world coaching leaders in business, health and education. He is co-director of The Happiness Project, a psychology based programme promoting success and happiness in life, work and relationships.

For further information on the work of Ben Renshaw and for details on public workshops, including the *Relationship Intelligence* seminar, contact:

Ben Renshaw
Clifton Gate
Clifton Avenue
London W12 9DR
Tel: 020 8762 0176
Fax: 020 8762 0176
E-mail: info@benrenshaw.com
Web site: www.happiness.co.uk

For further information about The Happiness Project and for details about 1) public workshops; 2) books and tapes; 3) Happiness NOW – the 8-Week Happiness Programme; 4) Teaching Happiness – The Certificate Training for trainers; 5) Coaching Success; 6) corporate seminars, contact:

The Happiness Project
Elms Court
Chapel Way
Oxford OX2 9LP
Tel: 01865 244414
Fax: 01865 248825
E-mail: hello@happiness.co.uk
Web site: www.happiness.co.uk

Suggested Reading

A Course in Miracles. Penguin Arkana, 1975

Beattie, Melody. Codependent No More. Hazelden, 1987

Canfield, Jack, Mark Victor Hansen, Mark & Chrissy Donnelly and Barbara De Angelis. Chicken Soup for the Couple's Soul. Vermilion, 1999

Carlson, Richard. Don't Sweat the Small Stuff in Love. Hodder & Stoughton, 1999

Carpenter, Tom. Dialogue on Awakening. Carpenter Press, 1992

Chopra, Deepak. The Path To Love. Rider, 1997

Covey, Stephen. The 7 Habits of Highly Effective People. Simon & Schuster, 1989

Dyer, Wayne. Your Sacred Self. Harper Collins, 1995

Frankl, Viktor. Man's Search for Meaning. Washington Square Press, 1984

Holden, Miranda. Relationships and Enlightenment. THP, 1997

Holden, Robert. Shift Happens! Hodder & Stoughton, 2000

Jeffers, Susan. Feel the Fear and Do It Anyway. Rider, 1991

Levine, Stephen & Ondrea. Embracing The Beloved. Gateway, 1995

McGraw, Phillip C. Relationship Rescue. Vermilion, 2000

Peck, Scott. The Road Less Travelled. Rider, 1978

Renshaw, Ben. Successful But Something Missing. Rider, 2000

Spezzano, Chuck. Wholeheartedness: Healing our Heartbreaks. Hodder & Stoughton, 2000

Walsch, Neale Donald. Conversations with God, Book 1. Hodder & Stoughton, 1997

Williams, Nick. The Work We Were Born To Do. Element, 2000

Williamson, Marianne. A Return to Love. Thorsons, 1992

Wilson, Paul. Calm for Life. Penguin 2000

Zohar, Danah and Marshall, Ian. SQ – Spiritual Intelligence The Ultimate Intelligence. Bloomsbury, 2000